LITE R ED

art&
music

LITERATURE-BASED

art&
music

CHILDREN'S BOOKS & ACTIVITIES TO ENRICH THE K-5 CURRICULUM

Mildred Knight Laughlin & Terri Parker Street

ORYX PRESS 1992

The rare Arabian Oryx is believed to have inspired the myth of the unicorn. This desert antelope became virtually extinct in the early 1960s. At that time several groups of international conservationists arranged to have 9 animals sent to the Phoenix Zoo to be the nucleus of a captive breeding herd. Today the Oryx population is nearly 800, and over 400 have been returned to reserves in the Middle East.

Copyright © 1992 by The Oryx Press
4041 North Central at Indian School Road
Phoenix, Arizona 85012-3397

Published simultaneously in Canada

Printed and Bound in the United States of America

∞ The paper used in this publication meets the minimum requirements of American National Standard for Information Science—Permanence of Paper for Printed Library Materials, ANSI Z39.48, 1984.

Library of Congress Cataloging-in-Publication Data
Laughlin, Mildred.
  Literature-based art and music : children's books and activities
to enrich the K–5 curriculum / by Mildred Knight Laughlin and Terri
Parker Street.
    p.   cm.
  Includes bibliographical references and index
  ISBN 0-89774-661-9.
  1. Arts—Study and teaching (Elementary)—United States.
2. Education, Elementary—United States—Activity programs.
3. Children's literature—Interpretation.   I. Street, Terri Parker.
II. Title.
NX303.L38   1992
372.5'044—dc20   91-33662
                                                          CIP
                                                          AC

For Mildred's daughters
Barbara and Debra
and
Terri's believers
Ken and Joan

CONTENTS

Introduction: Using Children's Literature in the Teaching of Art and Music

THEORETICAL BACKGROUND FOR CHOICE OF UNITS AND OBJECTIVES

Thirty years ago the Educational Policies Commission of the National Education Association acknowledged the necessity of arts in education. "All the higher mental processes involve more than the simple awareness of facts; they depend also on the ability *to conceive what might be,* as well as what is, to construct mental images in new and original ways. Experiences in literature and the arts may well make a larger contribution to those abilities than studies usually assumed to develop abstract thinking."[1] This great challenge to develop the aesthetic capabilities of children has increased in importance through the years. Regardless of the approach to teaching elementary school art and music, the literature-based method which this book utilizes will enrich the total program. Children must have access to library materials in order to encourage individual exploration and to integrate the arts into the remainder of the curriculum.

In the development of this work the authors found a number of children's books to enrich the K-5 art and music curricula. It was not difficult to develop enjoyable sharing activities because the books have significant content and are quality literature in their own right. The challenge was to develop units of study which were common to many art and music programs, for the methodologies in these areas, particularly music, are numerous and disparate. The problem was further compounded by the realization that many school districts lack specialists in art and music, so the responsibility for aesthetic education lies solely with the classroom teacher.

Many methodologies and curricular programs were examined by the authors, and scope and sequence charts were compared and analyzed. The most common area of agreement among program planners in both art and music was the necessity for active involvement by students in production, not merely in appreciation. As Bessie Swanson states, "Television has converted young and old alike into passive spectators. Because they have not developed resources within themselves, many people find their chief diversion in what is done *for* them."[2] It was the authors' intent to develop units in art and music which encourage active participation and higher order thinking skills, essential to an integrated approach to learning.

In preparing the units and objectives for this work, the authors were mindful of the spiral nature of learning. Objectives that were deemed most fundamental are included in the Kindergarten/Transition/First Grade units. These objectives are often expanded and built upon at higher levels. The authors realize that not all concepts and objectives in art and music lend themselves to the literature-based approach, often because quality literature to support those objectives is simply unavailable. Therefore, the units and objectives presented range across the curriculum but are not totally comprehensive.

After determining the units, objectives, and recommended readings, the authors developed activities that were pleasurable and worthwhile. It was the authors' desire to restore each child to the role of creator and performer; hence, many activities are product oriented. For the visual arts basic vehicles for learning that were utilized include collage, watercolor, sculpture, drawing, and creative writing. For music the activities are eclectic in nature and include body movement, critical listening, choral reading, creative dramatics, and art activities in addition to singing and performing on instruments. All the activities in this work were field-tested to insure practicality and ease of use by classroom teachers or curriculum specialists. The users of this book will find its units, objectives, and activities designed to meet their needs.

HOW THIS BOOK IS ORGANIZED AND HOW IT CAN BE USED

The units that follow provide suggested ideas for extending the art and music curricula beyond the scope and sequence that may have been developed in the local school district or at the state level. Selecting units that fit every curriculum at all times is impossible, but the concepts presented are basic and are commonly found in the scope and sequences of many curricula. The activities in many of the units are too long to be completed in one class period. Since class length and frequency of meetings varies among school districts, individual teachers will need to adapt the activities to meet the constraints of their particular schedules.

The units developed for each grade level are organized in a similar pattern. Each individual unit identifies objectives to be accomplished by using the trade books suggested. The objectives are written to be behavioral outcomes for students which teachers may use when preparing lesson plans. Knowledge and comprehension skills are basic for the objectives. Higher cognitive levels of appreciation, analysis, synthesis, and evaluation become more evident as progress through the grades is made. Each unit for both art and music includes a bibliography of recommended readings, provides a teacher or school library media specialist with an introductory activity, and suggests follow-up activities for teachers and students to share.

For kindergarten, transition, and first grade, the teacher will read books aloud and will direct activities. The brief annotations for the recommended books are descriptive in nature, as the activity related to the book provides a more detailed use guide. The objectives to be achieved by the activity are indicated following each annotation.

In the second- and third-grade units, many of the suggested activities are more self-directed and demand creative responses. Children may be asked to do research in the library media center, to practice listening and observation skills, or use creative dramatics. The activities are designed for a variety of levels of ability, and teachers should choose ones appropriate for their classes.

The units developed for grades four and five demand more self-directed work. Only a few books are suggested to be read aloud by the teacher. Teachers will introduce the books and children will carry out appropriate activities. Many times students are encouraged to complete research activities and accept the responsibility of sharing their findings with the other students. Many of the follow-up activities provide a variety of decision-making opportunities. The follow-up activities for individual or small groups may be accomplished with little or no teacher direction.

REFERENCES

1. Educational Policies Commission, "The Central Purpose of American Education." (Washington, DC: NEA, 1961), p. 18.
2. Bessie Swanson, *Music in the Education of Children, 3rd edition.* (Belmont, CA: Wadsworth, 1969), p. 6.

PART I
Art Programs

Chapter 1
Art: Kindergarten/ Transition/First Grade

Color

OBJECTIVES:

1. Identify and name the primary and secondary colors.
2. Recognize which specific colors combine to form secondary colors.
3. Show how color occurs in the environment.
4. Distinguish between light and dark values of a color.
5. Understand that use of black and white achieves maximum contrast.

RECOMMENDED READINGS:

Ehlert, Lois. *Planting a Rainbow.* Harcourt Brace Jovanovich, 1988.
Colorful graphics show flower seeds that are planted and grow into a spectrum of colors. (Objectives 3 and 4)

Hoban, Tana. *A, B, See!* Greenwillow, 1982.
Photograms depict objects in alphabetical order. (Objective 5)

Jonas, Ann. *Round Trip.* William Morrow, 1983.
Black-and-white graphics illustrate a trip to the city with the return trip and text displayed when the book is inverted and read back to front. (Objective 5)

Konigsburg, E. L. *Samuel Todd's Book of Great Colors.* Atheneum, 1990.
Objects that represent a variety of colors are introduced. (Objectives 1 and 3)

Lionni, Leo. *Little Blue and Little Yellow.* Astor, 1959.
When a spot of blue and one of yellow hug each other and turn green, their parents do not know them. (Objectives 1 and 2)

McMillan, Bruce. *Growing Colors.* Lothrop, Lee & Shepard, 1988.
With a text identifying color only, close-up photographs of individual fruits and vegetables are paired with an illustration of how each grows. (Objectives 1 and 3)

Reiss, John J. *Colors.* Bradbury, 1969.
Illustrated objects demonstrate tints and shades of primary and secondary colors as well as brown and black. (Objectives 1 and 4)

Walsh, Ellen Stoll. *Mouse Paint.* Harcourt Brace Jovanovich, 1989.
Jars of red, blue, and yellow paint are the source for an exploration of color by three white mice. (Objectives 1 and 2)

Zolotow, Charlotte. *Mr. Rabbit and the Lovely Present.* Illustrated by Maurice Sendak. Harper & Row, 1962.
A life-size rabbit helps a little girl decide on the perfect "color" present for her mother's birthday. (Objectives 1 and 3)

————. *Some Things Go Together.* Illustrated by Karen Gundersheimer. Thomas Y. Crowell, 1969, 1983.
Illustrated couplets identify objects and concepts that go together. (Objective 3)

GROUP INTRODUCTORY ACTIVITY:

Preparation: Locate Ellen Walsh's *Mouse Paint.* Cover a bulletin board with white paper. Cut a large white mouse outlined in pink (like Walsh's mice) and place it on one corner of the board. Cut three or more pairs of mouse footprints from sponge or styrofoam. Make them in a size proportional to the mouse on the board and similar to those on the endpapers of the book. Prepare trays with red, yellow, and blue tempera. Experiment with the various shades of these colors that are available to find those which blend best, since different companies use different pigments and yield more or less satisfactory results when combined.

Focus: Show the children the trays of tempera. Have them name the colors. Tell them that these are the primary colors and when they are mixed, they form secondary colors. Write the three primary colors on the chalkboard as the points of a triangle. Draw the triangle that connects the points.

Objective: To satisfy the objectives of naming primary colors and identifying how they combine to form secondary colors, tell the students that, as Ellen Walsh's *Mouse Paint* is read, they will find out what colors are made when any two of the three primary colors are mixed.

Guided Activity: After reading Walsh's book, have the students name the three secondary colors the mice made by blending any two primary colors. Write these on the appropriate line of the triangle on the board.

Extending Activity: Lightly draw six circles on a large sheet of white paper. In every other circle drop a small puddle of thin red, blue, or yellow tempera (a different color in each). Let students work two or four at a time with the stamps to make mouse prints leading toward an empty circle between two primary colors. When the two primary colors "meet" in the circle, let the children do a mouse dance with their stamps to mix and blend the paints into a secondary color. When through, have each child stamp the mouse footprint repeatedly on a piece of newsprint until it no longer prints, then give it to another student. When the color wheel is complete and dry, hang it on the bulletin board beside the white mouse with a caption such as, "*Mouse Paint:* Exploring the World of Color."

FOLLOW-UP ACTIVITIES FOR TEACHER AND STUDENTS TO SHARE:

1. Before introducing Lois Ehlert's *Planting a Rainbow*, show the class a bouquet of real or artificial flowers in varied colors. Have students identify the flowers and the colors. Share the book, talking about the bulbs planted in the fall and the seeds planted in the spring. Call attention to the name of each flower. As a follow-up activity, let the children make a collage rainbow mural using pictures cut from seed catalogs. While arranging the mural, discuss the light and dark values of each color. After the mural is completed, urge children to name the flowers and locate those that were pictured by Ehlert.
2. Share Tana Hoban's *A, B, See!* with the class. Have the students identify the objects on each page and then suggest which contrasts the most sharply with the black background. Let each child select a jelly bean from a dish. Have them place the jelly bean on a large sheet of black construction paper that has been spread with glue or spray adhesive. After each child has taken a turn, let the class identify

which colors contrast most drastically with the background. Note that lighter values have more contrast; therefore, white, the lightest value of all, is most different from the black background. As the children discuss, let them each select another jelly bean to eat.

3. Read Ann Jonas's *Round Trip* to the class. Show several double-spread pages and see if the children can recall what picture was made when the book was turned upside down. Point out that Jonas used black and white in order to achieve the greatest amount of contrast in her graphics. Let the children explore contrast by giving each of them half sheets of yellow and black construction paper. Have them cut out small white paper shapes and arrange them first on the yellow and then on the black paper. Let them paste their shapes on the background they feel gives the most contrast.

4. Before reading *Samuel Todd's Book of Great Colors* by E. L. Konigsburg, have the children review the primary and secondary colors and predict what other colors Konigsburg may have chosen as "great." After reading the book to the class, have the children recall the objects Konigsburg used to illustrate the primary and secondary colors. Have a "Great Colors" election. Let each child verbally complete the sentence, "My favorite color is because..." After these "campaign speeches" are completed, give each child a blank piece of paper for a ballot. Instruct them to use their favorite color of crayon to mark an "X" on their ballots. Tell the class that in elections people can only vote one time, so they must only put one "X" on their ballots. Have them place the completed ballots in a box. Select a child to "read" the ballots as the results are tallied and graphed on the board. Examine the results to see if the three class favorites were primary colors, secondary colors, or neither.

5. Read aloud Leo Lionni's *Little Blue and Little Yellow*. Remind the class that blue and yellow are two of the primary colors. Let the children name the third primary color. Ask what would have happened if Little Blue met Little Red instead of Little Yellow or if Little Red met Little Yellow. Create a language experience story called "Little Blue and His Friends." Begin with the plot of Lionni's book and urge children to think of other ways the colors might meet. For example, Little Red and Little Blue might run into each other at a corner and hit so hard that they combine to make purple. After all the secondary colors have been formed, illustrate the story with pieces of colored transparency film which can be overlapped to make the secondary colors.

6. Before reading Bruce McMillan's *Growing Colors*, explain to the children that the illustrations were taken after each vegetable or fruit was sprayed with water because colors in nature look best when wet with rain. Tell the children that both primary and secondary colors are represented in the fruits and vegetables McMillan used. Have the class recall the primary and secondary colors and predict what fruits and vegetables the author photographed to illustrate each. Record their predictions on the board. Read the book, having the children identify the color word, name the vegetable or fruit representing that color, and tell how it grows in relationship to the ground. When the book is completed, let the children identify the primary and secondary color objects McMillan photographed. Compare these with the predictions the children made earlier. As a follow-up activity let each student choose a favorite fruit or vegetable from a seed catalog, cut it out, and paste it on a sheet of white paper. Let the child label the object and the color represented, helping as needed. Compile these into a *My Favorite Food* book.

7. Share each double-spread page of John Reiss's *Colors*. Let the class identify the objects and point out the light and dark values of the colors. Have the children note which objects this author used to depict primary and secondary colors. Turn to the title page and let the children examine the illustrated color quilt. Have them point out the various shades of colors. Distribute four-inch squares of white paper to the children. Divide the class into six committees, giving each a different primary or secondary color. Have them select from their crayons shades and tints of their assigned color and color their squares into solid-colored "quilt blocks." Some may want to use more or less pressure to achieve a lighter or darker value. Arrange and tape their squares onto a large sheet of butcher paper to make a class quilt.

8. Read Charlotte Zolotow's *Mr. Rabbit and the Lovely Present.* Let the children recall the primary color gifts the rabbit suggests might be given to the mother. Point out that Zolotow only used one secondary color, the one named by the little girl in the story. Have the children identify the two secondary colors Zolotow did not use and suggest gifts that could represent these colors. As a follow-up activity, have the children make small paper cone baskets by overlapping and gluing together two connecting sides of a paper square. Have each child draw flowers and leaf shapes to color in

primary and secondary colors. Let the children cut out and glue or tape the shapes to a straw or pipe cleaner stem. Arrange the flowers in the cone baskets for them to take home as a gift for a favorite person.

9. Introduce Charlotte Zolotow's *Some Things Go Together* by playing a brief word association game with the class. Ask the group to respond with the first thing they think of when a word is given. For example, if the word is "happy," they might reply "birthday." Do several pairings. Ask the students to listen for the colors and their pairings as they hear *Some Things Go Together*. After reading the book, have students recall the color pairings they heard.

Tell students that colors can also be associated with feelings. To illustrate this concept play the word association game again. Tell the children that this time the words given will be about feelings, such as "happy," "angry," and "sad." Ask them to respond with the color they think of when they hear each "feeling" word.

Shape

OBJECTIVES:

1. Identify and name geometric shapes.
2. Recognize that shapes are created when the ends of a line are joined.
3. Demonstrate the use of geometric shapes to create variety and repetition.
4. Recognize the use of positive and negative shapes to form patterns, objects, and designs.
5. Note shapes as they occur in the environment.

RECOMMENDED READINGS:

Ehlert, Lois. *Color Zoo.* J. B. Lippincott, 1989.
Colors and shapes are emphasized as overlapping animal faces are created. (Objectives 1 and 4)
Emberley, Ed. *Picture Pie.* Little, Brown, 1984.
Illustrations demonstrate how circles can be cut into wedges and used to create animals, plants, other objects, and designs. (Objectives 3 and 4)

————. *The Wing on a Flea.* Little, Brown. 1961.
Line drawings enhance the poetry that humorously identifies unusual triangular, rectangular, and circular shapes in the environment. (Objectives 3 and 4)

Fisher, Leonard Everett. *Look Around!* Viking Kestrel, 1987.
Simple text defines each of the four basic illustrated shapes and provides examples. (Objectives 1, 2, and 5)

Gardner, Beau. *What Is It?* G. P. Putnam's Sons, 1989.
White graphics attached to the page can be rotated to resemble the objects pictured on the left. (Objective 4)

Hoban, Tana. *Circles, Triangles and Squares.* Macmillan, 1974.
In this wordless book black-and-white photographs depict shapes in the environment. (Objectives 1 and 5)

————. *Round & Round & Round.* Greenwillow, 1983.
Photographs of circular objects in the environment are included in this textless book. (Objectives 1 and 5)

————. *Shapes, Shapes, Shapes.* Greenwillow, 1986.
Photographs allow the reader to distinguish shapes that make up familiar objects. (Objectives 1 and 5)

Reiss, John J. *Shapes.* Bradbury, 1974.
Identified illustrations introduce squares, cubes, triangles, circles, spheres, rectangles, ovals, and more complicated shapes. (Objectives 1, 2, and 3)

GROUP INTRODUCTORY ACTIVITY:

Preparation: Locate *Look Around!* by Leonard Everett Fisher and a long length of lightweight rope or elastic (about 24 feet).

Focus: Introduce Fisher's book by asking students to name the various shapes they know. Point out that shapes are all around us and some shapes are so common they have names of their own, e.g., triangles, circles, and squares.

Objective: To satisfy the objectives of identifying geometric shapes, naming them, and noting them as they occur in the environment, tell the children that Leonard Everett Fisher's *Look Around!* is about some of the most common shapes in our world. Ask them to listen as the book is read for the name of each of the shapes Fisher uses.

Guided Activity: After reading Fisher's book, have students name the shapes used. Write these on the board and draw a picture of each shape beside the name. The class or individual students may give verbal directions for drawing each figure. Let children name objects that contain each of the shapes and find examples of each in the classroom.

Extending Activity: Show the class the length of rope (or elastic) and point out that the rope is a line. Discuss with the children what could be done to make the rope into a shape and then tie the ends of the rope together. Have the class or a group of children stand and encircle them with the rope or elastic. Ask the children to put both hands on the rope and hold it so that it crosses their backs at the waist. Instruct the children to form a circle with the rope by moving themselves as necessary. The task will be easier if one child or a chair is designated as the center of the circle and the group is reminded that all parts of the circle are the same distance from the center. When this has been accomplished satisfactorily, have the group form other shapes by moving appropriately.

FOLLOW-UP ACTIVITIES FOR TEACHER AND STUDENTS TO SHARE:

1. Introduce Lois Ehlert's *Color Zoo* by holding up objects or cut-outs of the basic shapes Ehlert used. Ask the children to identify each shape. Then read the book and let the children identify the shapes Ehlert used to make each animal. As a follow-up let the children use attribute blocks or cut-out shapes to form animals or creative pictures. If cut-out shapes are used, they may want to glue them into position for display.

2. Introduce Ed Emberley's *Picture Pie* by using a flannelboard on which eight wedges are assembled to form a circle. Read the first two pages of the text. Manipulate the pieces on the flannelboard to duplicate some of the illustrations in the book. Leaf through the book to show children some of the pictures and designs that can be created with circles and portions of circles. Place the flannelboard, additional circles and wedges in a variety of colors, and Emberley's book in a reading or art area. Encourage children to go to the area, look at the book, and duplicate some of Emberley's designs or create their own.

3. Before reading Ed Emberley's *The Wing on a Flea*, tell the children that, after the book is read, they will be asked to recall the objects identified as having specific shapes. After they identify as many as possible, review the pictures so students may locate any objects that were forgotten. As a follow-up, use the last four lines in the book to caption a bulletin board on which the children arrange cut-out shapes to form objects such as snowmen, houses, mountains, and trees.

4. Share Beau Gardner's *What Is It?* by covering the left side of each page and rotating the movable graphic on the right. Let the children try to identify the shapes at different locations on the page. After they view the shapes imaginatively, remove the cover from the left side of the page and see Gardner's identification. As an extending activity place on the overhead projector object shapes that were previously cut from a coloring book. Let the children identify the objects, using only the outline of the projected shapes as a clue.

5. Before sharing Tana Hoban's *Circles, Triangles and Squares*, cut a circle, triangle, and square from construction paper and have the children identify the shapes. Tell them that all three shapes will be found in Hoban's book. They will be asked to name the shapes pictured on each page and discuss the environment in which those shapes occurred. As a follow-up activity, have the children fold paper hats in triangle shapes. As the folding is carried out, ask the class to identify the new shapes that evolve during the process. After the hats are completed, read Esphyr Slobodkina's *Caps for Sale* (Harper & Row, 1940) aloud to the class. Ask all the children except one to be monkeys and the remaining one to be the peddler. Play out the story, beginning with the scene where the peddler awakens from his nap. As a treat, follow the dramatics by having the children each select two matching crackers from a tray of crackers in different shapes and make a peanut butter cracker sandwich.

6. Introduce Tana Hoban's *Round & Round & Round* by letting the class identify all the objects they can think of that are round. List the objects on the blackboard. Share Hoban's photographs and let children identify the round objects that are illustrated. Add to the list any not already mentioned. As a follow-up, give the children old magazines from which they can each cut out a round object. Let them glue the picture to a sheet of paper on the top of which has been duplicated, "Round as a _____." With the teacher's assistance as needed, the child can fill in the blank appropriately for his or her picture. Compile the sheets into a *Round As* book to keep in the art area. As a further activity with round, let the children bring from home a round toy or one that has round parts. Let each child demonstrate how he or she plays with the toy. After each demonstration, let the class discuss whether the toy would operate successfully if it were a different shape. Set up a "round toy" display in the classroom with each child's name identifying his or her toy.

7. Before sharing Tana Hoban's *Shapes, Shapes, Shapes,* prepare an overhead transparency of the shapes Hoban notes on the introductory page. Share Hoban's page, letting the children identify the shapes and learn new ones. Then, as the textless pages are shared, project the transparency so the children can refer to the shapes as they try to identify the many that are illustrated in the photographs. More than one day will be needed to share the photographs, allowing a review of the shape names illustrated on the overhead. After sharing the book, take a walk around the school yard (or around the neighborhood if volunteer adults or upper grade students are available). Record the shapes children see in the familiar objects in the environment.

8. Introduce John Reiss's *Shapes* by allowing children to identify the objects which illustrate the shapes. As a follow-up give each child a strip of paper with the five lines of the music staff drawn on it and eight to twelve black ovals to represent the notes. Let each child place the ovals on the staff to create individual melodies. Have each student draw stems on the ovals to make notes. If desired, the teacher can then play each child's created tune on a keyboard, xylophone, or other available instrument. As each is played the children may wish to accompany on instruments representing shapes, i.e., triangles; tambourines, drums, or finger cymbals for circles; woodblocks or sandblocks for rectangles, etc.

Line and Texture

OBJECTIVES:

1. Identify varieties of lines.
2. Recognize various line directions.
3. Realize that repeating lines form patterns.
4 See that the contour of a shape can be drawn as a line.
5. Identify various textures through tactile stimulation.
6. Distinguish various textures visually.

RECOMMENDED READINGS:

Carle, Eric. *The Very Busy Spider.* Philomel, 1985.
The tactile format enhances the story of a spider who refuses to be distracted from spinning her web. (Objectives 2, 3, and 5)

Freeman, Don. *Corduroy.* Viking, 1968.
A teddy bear dressed in corduroy overalls searches a department store for his missing button and finally finds a friend. (Objectives 3 and 6)

Hoban, Tana. *Dots, Spots, Speckles, and Stripes.* Greenwillow, 1987.
Stripes in the environment can be identified in this textless book of photographs. (Objectives 2 and 3)

————. *Is It Rough? Is It Smooth? Is It Shiny?* Greenwillow, 1984.
Photographs depict various textures found in common objects. (Objective 6)

————. *Look! Look! Look!* Greenwillow, 1988.
Portions of a photographed object can be viewed through a small cut-out hole before the entire object is revealed. (Objectives 1, 3, and 6)

Johnson, Crockett. *Harold and the Purple Crayon.* Harper & Row, 1955.
Crayon lines create the pathway and the objects Harold sees on his fantasy walk. (Objectives 1, 2, 3, and 4)

Pluckrose, Henry. *Pattern.* Illustrated by Chris Fairclough. Franklin Watts, 1988.
Illustrations and brief text point out that colors, lines, and shapes form patterns. (Objectives 1, 2, and 3)

Robbins, Ken. *City/Country.* Viking, 1985.
Photographs of a car trip reveal a variety of lines in the environment. (Objectives 1, 2, and 3)

Yashima, Taro. *Umbrella.* Viking, 1958.
Lines are featured in the illustrations as three-year-old Momo tries out her umbrella and red boots in the rain. (Objectives 2 and 3)

GROUP INTRODUCTORY ACTIVITY:

Preparation: Locate *Look! Look! Look!* by Tana Hoban. Collect some of the objects illustrated in the book to share with the class. Hoban used a cover sheet in front of each illustration. This sheet contained a circular hole which allowed only a portion of each photograph to be visible. Because students will be using a similar approach in creating their own book, prepare a shape pattern around which children can trace the outline for the hole in each of the cover sheets.

Focus: Introduce Tana Hoban's *Look! Look! Look!* by showing the children the small portion of the photograph revealed by the cut-out page. Let students try to identify the object. Show the class the complete photograph of the dog.

Objective: In order to fulfill the objectives of identifying varieties of lines, realizing that repeating lines form patterns, and distinguishing various textures visually, turn back to the cut-out page. Ask the class what clues helped them identify the object. Summarize their responses and point out that line directions, patterns, and texture all give clues to the identity of the whole object.

Guided Activity: Ask the children to focus on lines, patterns, and textures as they view the partial photographs on the succeeding pages of Hoban's book before seeing the whole object. Share the book, allowing students to suggest potential objects on each cut-out page. After the students suggest possibilities, ask them to describe how the object would feel if they could touch it. Turn the page to reveal the photograph of the actual object. Students may now want to change or add to their description of the texture. Share the entire book, turning back to the cut-out page each time to elicit the children's ideas about clues used in identification. Display some of the objects that Hoban photographed. Allow the children to feel the objects and then add to or change their earlier observations of texture if they desire. Note any differences between the visual and tactile textures of the objects.

Extending Activity: Prior to the activity collect old magazines with a variety of large colorful illustrations. Allow children to select a single picture from the magazines and cut it out. To simplify this step the students may choose illustrations from a prepared group of pictures. Also prepare two sheets of 8" x 8" white paper for each child. Lightweight card stock is preferable, but heavy typing paper will do. Allow each child to carefully glue the chosen picture on one sheet of paper. Trace around a prepared shape pattern on the second sheet. Let each child carefully cut out the shape and place the second sheet over the first to create "peek hole" overlays like Hoban used. Trim any rough edges and compile into a *Look and See* book.

FOLLOW-UP ACTIVITIES FOR TEACHER AND STUDENTS TO SHARE:

1. Read Eric Carle's *The Very Busy Spider* to the class. After completing the story, pass the book around the group so each child may feel the raised texture of the web. Talk about real spider webs and their texture. Ask the children what materials might be used to make a

spider web. Let the children create their own webs. Suggested materials and methods include:

   a. Rubber bands on geoboards,

   b. Yarn or string glued to paper, and

   c. Glue applied to scraps of laminating film or waxed paper.

    In method c children should first use a dark crayon to draw their webs on paper. Place and secure the film or waxed paper over the drawing. The children should then use glue dispensed from small-nozzled bottles to trace their webs. When the webs dry, the film or paper may be carefully peeled from them. The finished products will adhere to windows or other smooth surfaces where they can be arranged to form tactile displays. *Warning:* If the glue webs are left in place for extended periods of time, they lose their elasticity and will have to be lightly scraped from the surface. This is especially true if they are exposed to high heat or intense sunlight.

2. Introduce Don Freeman's *Corduroy* by showing the children a variety of fabric scraps with differing textures, such as corduroy, silk, cotton, burlap, felt, and velvet. Let the children touch the cloth and describe the various textures. Show the illustration in Freeman's *Corduroy* when the little bear realizes he has lost his button. Ask the children if they know why the book is titled *Corduroy*. Point out the pattern of vertical stripes that is characteristic of corduroy fabric. Read the story.

    Tell the children that, even though Corduroy has Lisa, he might like to have another friend, especially a little bear that is like him. Give each child an 8½" x 11" sheet of brown construction paper and ask each student to draw a teddy bear shape on the paper. Have the children cut out the bears. Have each child choose a fabric scrap for his or her bear. Let the children cut out clothing to glue onto their bears to create friends for Corduroy. When all have dressed their bears, let the children name them to correspond with the name or texture of the material used.

3. Before sharing Tana Hoban's *Dots, Spots, Speckles, and Stripes*, introduce the concept of stripes as representing lines that can be horizontal, vertical, or diagonal. Have the children think of striped objects. List their responses on the board. Tell the children that, as the pictures in Tana Hoban's book are shared, they are to watch for striped objects to add to their list. After sharing the book, record on the blackboard the striped objects the students recall. Ask the class if Hoban's pictures made them think of any additional objects that are striped. Read the list and let the children classify the stripes in each object as either horizontal, vertical, diagonal, or multi-directional.

As a reminder for the follow-up activity, let the children look again at the photograph of the kitten and the tennis shoe. Give each child a cut-out of a tennis shoe with pre-punched holes for laces. Let each class member design his or her own striped pattern for the tennis shoe. Allow each child to choose cut lengths of yarn in a favorite color to lace the shoes. It may be necessary to number the holes and give directions for either horizontal or diagonal lacing.

4. Before sharing Tana Hoban's *Is It Rough? Is It Smooth? Is It Shiny?*, have the class brainstorm terms that indicate how objects feel to the touch, such as "rough," "smooth," "sticky," "soft," "slick." Tell the children that the title includes the word "shiny." It describes how something *looks,* not how something feels. To illustrate the concept share two pennies, one shiny and one dull. Ask one child to feel both pennies without looking at them. Ask if they feel the same. Show the class the pennies and point out that both pennies feel the same even though they look different. Since "shiny" is not a texture word, ask the children to disregard that term as they view the book. Show each illustration to the class and ask the students to identify the item and the texture of each. Before class prepare a sack with a variety of small objects, such as a paper clip, a cotton ball, a clothes pin, a tennis ball. Have a child reach into the sack, find an object, identify its texture, and try to name it before bringing it out of the sack. Let that child show the object to the class so the group can verify or negate the decision. Continue the activity until all children have had the tactile experience of identifying an unseen object.

5. Before reading *Harold and the Purple Crayon* by Crockett Johnson, ask the children to recall what they know about the kinds of lines (e.g., straight, curved, dotted) and the directions they can take (horizontal, vertical, and diagonal). Tell them that in Crockett Johnson's book Harold uses a crayon to draw the objects he sees on an imaginary walk. Suggest that, as the book is read, the class should note the varieties and directions of the lines Harold used. After reading the story, let children discuss the lines they saw. Note patterns made by repeating lines, e.g., the waves, windows, dragon's teeth. As a follow-up have each child select a favorite color crayon and make a line drawing of an object he or she would most like to have. Assist each child to label his or her picture. Compile the illustrations in a *My Magic Crayon* book.

6. Prior to reading *Pattern* by Henry Pluckrose, ask the children if they know what the term "pattern" means. Record their definitions on the board. Read *Pattern*, having the children point out the patterns they

see on each page. Discuss whether the patterns are identifiable because of color, line, or shape. After discussing each page, reexamine the illustrations. Note whether straight lines, curved, or a combination of both are used in each pattern. Draw attention to the zig-zig lines in the black-and-white "checkerboard" pattern. As a follow-up, have children in one group experiment with creating a pattern with Legos while each child in the other group uses crayons to create an individual pattern by using one of his or her printed initials. The children may want to use the page of "A's" as a guideline. Let all the children participate in both activities.

7. Have the children close their eyes and think about riding in a car down the street. What kinds of lines and line directions do they see, e.g., up and down, across, slanted, curved, straight, dotted? Introduce the more appropriate terms vertical, horizontal, and diagonal for the directional words. As the children suggest a type of line, have them identify the object or place where they imagine that line can be seen. Tell the children that as Ken Robbins's *City/Country*, a car trip in photographs, is read aloud, they are to notice the varieties and directions of the lines and the shapes or patterns they make. After reading the book, let the children recall the types and directions of the lines seen and the shapes made. Examine the pictures again so children may discover any lines they may not have noticed, e.g., the curved, dotted lines formed by the lights in the tunnel.

  As a follow-up activity ask upper-grade volunteers to assist the class, in small groups, to take a walk around the block to look for lines. Stop several times so the volunteers can record both the lines children notice at a particular location and the object containing those lines. Return to the classroom and let each group share their findings. Make a pictograph of the results by illustrating the types of lines down the side of the blackboard (for the y-axis) and horizontally graphing the responses from the committees (along the x-axis) that evidence that type of line. Tell the children that their lines have now formed a pictograph and explain the term.

8. Introduce Taro Yashima's *Umbrella* by discussing how lines can be used to illustrate various weather conditions. Ask a child to volunteer to make rain lines on the blackboard. After the lines are drawn, ask the children whether the wind was blowing when that rain was falling. Have another child show how the lines would look in a bad, windy storm. Discuss what types of lines would show lightning, clouds, and sunshine. Allow volunteers to add each of these to the board. Tell the class that Taro Yashima dedicated this story to his

daughter Momo. It illustrates her as she tries out her new red boots and umbrella in a rainstorm. Ask the students to watch how Yashima used lines to show the rain as Momo walks home with her father. After reading the story, compare the lines Yashima used for the rain with those drawn by the children. Also call attention to the Japanese character for "rain."

As a follow-up, let children make crayon scratchboard weather pictures. Have children choose wax crayons and heavily color an entire sheet of paper. Mix a small amount of liquid detergent with black tempera paint in a ratio of about one part detergent to eight parts tempera and allow each child to paint over his or her entire paper. The detergent will allow the paint to cover and adhere to the crayoned page. When the paint is thoroughly dry, each child may scratch his or her weather picture into the paint with a stylus, pencil, or other instrument, revealing the bright crayon beneath. Group the pictures together in an area titled "Walking in the Rain." As a musical follow-up to this activity, go back to the page where Yashima says, "On the umbrella, raindrops made a wonderful music. . ." Let the children perform a body percussion rainstorm as the text is read. They may lightly clap the rhythm of the words "Bon polo," pat their legs to the rhythm of "ponpolo ponpolo," and lightly stamp their feet for "bolo boto ponpolo" and "boto boto ponpolo." Reverse the words as the storm lessens. If xylophones are available, one child may be selected to improvise a rain melody with those rhythms while the rest of the class provides the body percussion.

Space

OBJECTIVES:

1. Determine the relationship between a figure and the background.
2. Identify depth by overlapping.
3. Distinguish depth by size of shapes.
4. Recognize the horizon as separating the main divisions of space.

RECOMMENDED READINGS:

Brett, Jan. *Annie and the Wild Animals.*˙ Houghton Mifflin, 1985.
Bordered illustrations enhance the story of Annie's search for a pet to replace her lost cat. (Objectives 1 and 2)

Crews, Donald. *School Bus.* Greenwillow, 1984.
Position on the pages gives depth to the illustrations of school buses transporting children back and forth to school. (Objective 2)

Gillham, Bill. *Can You See It?* Illustrated by Fiona Horne. G.P. Putnam's Sons, 1986.
Close-up photographs illustrate objects that children may find on the succeeding page. (Objective 1)

Jonas, Ann. *The Trek.* Greenwillow, 1985.
Real-life objects become hidden animals to a little girl as she walks to school. (Objective 1)

Rylant, Cynthia. *Night in the Country.* Illustrated by Mary Szilagyi. Bradbury, 1986.
Colored-pencil illustrations of rural scenes depict a number of spatial concepts. (Objectives 1, 3, and 4)

Tafuri, Nancy. *All Year Long.* Greenwillow, 1983.
Depth is realized through the size of the shapes in graphic illustrations depicting various seasonal activities. (Objectives 3 and 4)

————. *Do Not Disturb.* Greenwillow, 1987.
Depth shown by size of shapes is apparent in this almost wordless story of a family who arouse the forest creatures while camping in the woods. (Objective 3)

————. *Follow Me!* Greenwillow, 1990.
A distinct line marks the horizon in many of the watercolor illustrations that tell the story of a young sea lion following a crab. (Objectives 3 and 4)

————. *Have You Seen My Duckling?* Greenwillow, 1984.
The other ducklings follow the mother duck as she searches for her missing baby. (Objective 1)

GROUP INTRODUCTORY ACTIVITY:

Preparation: Locate Cynthia Rylant's *Night in the Country.*

Focus: Tell the children they will hear *Night in the Country* by Cynthia Rylant so that they can enjoy the words and the illustrations. Then they will carefully look again at each picture to see how the artist made some parts seem closer to the reader than others appear to be.

Objective: Read the book to the class. In order to see the relationship between a figure and the background, to note depth by size of shapes, and to see the horizon as separating the main divisions of space, examine the double-spread illustration of the title page. Ask the children which tractor is closer, the one on the left or the one on the right? What clues helped the children decide? Ask children to locate where the sky begins and speculate about why the artist used red and yellow for this area.

Guided Activity: Turn to the succeeding page. In what way is the line where the sky meets the earth different from the skyline on the previous page? Introduce the term horizon by telling the class that the imaginary line where the earth and sky seem to meet is called the horizon. Talk about how the artist made the house with the red roof seem closer than the barn. Let a child describe the location of the house with the purple roof. After the children identify size as showing depth, turn to the next page and ask which owl seems closest to them. Again emphasize size to distinguish depth. Note the horizon again. In this picture it is not a clearly defined line. Continue examining the double-spread illustrations, letting the children identify which objects or animals seem closer to them. When it is appropriate, let them point out the horizon and describe the location of specific objects.

Extending Activity: Take the children to the playground or a nearby park. Have the class sit in a circle small enough so everyone can hear. Choose a highly visible object and ask children to describe its location in relation to another object in the background. Repeat this activity with different children and objects. Have the children turn around so they are facing outward from the circle. Let the children take turns describing the relationship between two objects they see. Ask the students to locate the horizon. Explain that the horizon is the point where the sky meets the trees, rooftops, etc. In order to extend the activity further and to reinforce the concept of using size to determine depth, select like objects of similar size, e.g., trees or houses.

FOLLOW-UP ACTIVITIES FOR TEACHER AND STUDENTS TO SHARE:

1. Read *Annie and the Wild Animals* by Jan Brett. Stop reading when Annie has run out of cornmeal and can make no more corn cakes. Let the children anticipate what has happened to Taffy. After the children have predicted, finish the story. Return to the beginning of the story. Draw students' attention to the illustrations in the border

and discuss how they add to the wintry feeling of the page. Focus on the border of each succeeding page and have children locate Taffy on each. Have children tell Taffy's story as it unfolds in the borders. Go through the story a third time, having the children identify the object that appears closest to the reader in each picture and the item that seems most distant. As a follow-up tell the class that overlapping objects give a sense of depth to a picture. Have a flannelboard with a variety of felt shapes representing trees and animals available in a learning center. Let children experiment with overlapping and positioning the shapes on the flannelboard to create a sense of depth.

2. Introduce the concept of overlapping to convey depth or proximity to the viewer by holding two small objects, one slightly closer to the class than the other. Ask the children which object is closer to them. Give the children the opportunity to discuss the reasons for their responses. Move one object until it overlaps the other. Let the children discuss which object now seems closer. Point out that the object in front of the other can be seen in its entirety while the other is partially hidden by the first. This overlapping enables the viewer to determine which object is closer. Share the picture of the yellow school buses, the first double-spread illustration in *School Bus* by Donald Crews. Ask the children if they can tell which buses seem the closest to them. How did they reach that decision? Read the rest of the book, having children notice depth through the overlapping of objects and people within the illustrations. When the page labeled "GO" is shared, call attention to the size of the pedestrians on the sidewalk. Note that, in order to make the individuals seem farther away, they are smaller. Continue reading *School Bus*, having children identify depth by overlapping or size of objects. As a follow-up, give each child an 8½" x 11" sheet of paper and ask the students to draw a school bus to color and cut out. Tell the class to imagine that their school buses have transported children to a large track meet. Have them make a collage with their buses that shows depth by overlapping.

3. Before sharing Bill Gillham's *Can You See It?*, tell the children to examine the close-up photographs carefully because they will need to locate the object on the succeeding page and describe it in relation to the background. Position one picture at a time under an opaque projector so all may see. Have students signal when they find the hidden object in the second of each pair of photographs. Choose one student to describe the location of the object, for example, "under the _____," "beside the _____," "behind the _____," etc. When the book

is completed, show the class several objects. Tell them that a duplicate of each object is hidden in the multi-purpose room, playground, or other selected location. Take the class to that location, display one object at a time, and have the children search for its hidden match. When a child locates the object, call the students together and let the child describe the location of the hidden object. See if another student can find the item from the description. Repeat the activity until all the hidden objects have been found.

4. Tell the children that in *The Trek* by Ann Jonas a little girl makes the ordinary walk to school more exciting by imagining hidden animals in the objects she passes. While reading the story, ask the children to identify the hidden animals on each page. Have them describe each one in relation to the rest of the picture. When the story is completed, use the "Animals We Know" chart on the final two pages to see which ones the children found. Tell the class the book will be in the reading corner so they may look for the animals they missed. As they find a hidden animal, they should share its location with the class.

5. Before sharing Nancy Tafuri's *All Year Long*, divide the children into pairs and give one child in each couple a cardboard cylinder from an empty toilet tissue roll. Give the other child an object to be viewed through the cylinder. Have the child holding the object slowly move it closer to and farther from the partner's tube as the partner watches through the cylinder. Ask the viewers to notice whether the object looks larger when it is close to the tube or when it is a distance from it. Exchange tasks so both children experience viewing the object. Tell the students that, as they look at the seasonal activities of a child in Tafuri's book, they are to examine the illustrations in order to see how the size of the shapes is used to create depth. Read the story, allowing children to comment and discuss depth and size of shapes in each illustration (e.g., the size of the boys relative to the house in the March picture or the size of the seed package in relation to the tree in the illustration for May). After the book is completed, go back through the illustrations so children may note those pictures where the horizon is clearly visible. Reinforce the term horizon as the line in the distance where the air and earth seem to meet.

6. Before sharing *Do Not Disturb* by Nancy Tafuri, tell the children that they will examine the illustrations to tell the textless portion of the story. Let the children participate in telling the story. Have them talk about the sounds each animal makes. Assign parts to create an animal chorus for the last page. After reading the story, urge the class to

discuss the phrase "Do not disturb" that Tafuri uses as the title. Go back through the book, asking the class to note how the size of shapes shows depth in the illustrations. Have the children also discover what animal is being disturbed on each page. As a follow-up activity, ask the children if they have ever stayed in a hotel or motel and seen a "Do not disturb" sign they can hang on the door. Give each child a piece of lightweight card stock on which the outline of a "Do not disturb" sign and the circle for the doorknob has been duplicated. Let each children print the words and decorate his or her own "Do not disturb" sign to take home.

7. Show the class the cover of Nancy Tafuri's *Follow Me!* Ask the children what they think the story is about. After some child identifies that it is about a sea lion, call the students' attention to the other sea lions on the cover. Ask why those sea lions are so much smaller than the one they noticed in the foreground. After students have identified size as denoting depth and distance, share Nancy Tafuri's book with the group. Have the children tell the textless story by "reading" the pictures. When the story is completed, urge them to examine the cover of the book again. Point out the sky. Ask the class if anyone recalls the name for the line that shows where the sky meets the water or land. If no one remembers, remind the class that the line formed where the sky and sea meet is called the horizon. Examine the pages again, having the children identify the horizon on each page where it occurs. Note the rocky islands in the distance that sometimes keep the horizon from being a straight line. Let the children discuss why some illustrations do not show the horizon. As a follow-up have the children draw the horizon line and a baby seal on a sheet of paper. Let each child paint his or her picture. Remind the children that the space above the line is sky and should be painted appropriately. Display the pictures along the wall or the top of the chalkboard so that the horizon lines match. Point out that the pictures themselves do not form a straight line because each child placed the horizon in a different position on the page.

8. Prior to sharing Nancy Tafuri's *Have You Seen My Duckling?*, explain to the class that there are very few words in the story and that they will need to read the pictures. Read the book. On the pages without words have the students tell the story from the pictures. Do not call attention to the hidden duckling on each page unless a child notices it. When the book is completed, reexamine the illustrations so the children may locate the duckling on each page, describe the duckling's activity, and note its position relative to the background (e.g., "across the pond" or "beside the turtle"). As a follow-up, give

each child an animal sticker. Have the children name the animals represented and discuss the environments where they might be found. Allow each child to position his or her sticker on a page of art paper and use crayons to hide the animal in an appropriate setting. Display the completed pictures on the bulletin board.

Media and Methods

OBJECTIVES:

1. Note crayon and colored pencil in illustrations.
2. Produce original crayon or colored pencil illustrations.
3. Recognize collage as a medium for illustration.
4. Create collage illustrations.
5. Recognize watercolor in illustrations.
6. Paint an original watercolor.

RECOMMENDED READINGS:

Baskin, Hosea, Tobias, and Lisa. *Hosie's Alphabet.* Illustrated by Leonard Baskin. Viking, 1972.
   Watercolor illustrations and descriptive language combine to form this striking alphabet book. (Objectives 5 and 6)
Carle, Eric. *The Mixed-Up Chameleon.* Thomas Y. Crowell, 1975, 1984.
   Collage pictures illustrate the humorous story of the chameleon who wished to be like someone else. (Objectives 3 and 4)
Keats, Ezra Jack. *Jennie's Hat.* Harper & Row, 1966.
   A variety of materials form the illustrations that extend the story of how the birds help Jennie to create a beautiful hat. (Objectives 3 and 4)
Lionni, Leo. *Alexander & the Wind-Up Mouse.* Pantheon, 1969.
   Newspaper, tissue paper, and patterned and marbleized papers are used to enhance the story of how Alexander makes a "real" friend from a wind-up mouse. (Objectives 3 and 4)
Marshall, James. *Goldilocks and the Three Bears.* Dial, 1988.
   Ink and watercolor illustrations extend in humorous fashion the author's version of the traditional tale. (Objectives 5 and 6)

Paterson, Bettina. *My First Animals.* Thomas Y. Crowell, 1990.
Layered paper collage is used to illustrate names of familiar animals.
(Objectives 3 and 4)

Rylant, Cynthia. *The Relatives Came.* Illustrated by Stephen Gammell.
Bradbury, 1985.
The distinctive strokes of the colored pencil lend texture to the illustrations, enhancing the story of the visit by the relatives from Virginia.
(Objectives 1 and 2)

——. *This Year's Garden.* Illustrated by Mary Szilagyi. Bradbury,1984.
Colored pencil drawings show the effect of the seasons of the year on the
family's garden. (Objectives 1 and 2)

Tafuri, Nancy. *Spots, Feathers, and Curly Tails.* Greenwillow, 1988.
Watercolor illustrations provide clues to answer the questions regarding
the characteristics of farm animals. (Objectives 5 and 6)

Weiss, Nicki. *Where Does the Brown Bear Go?* Greenwillow, 1989.
Colored pencil illustrations highlight the simple text of animals on their
way home when night comes. (Objectives 1 and 2)

GROUP INTRODUCTORY ACTIVITY:

Preparation: Locate *Where Does the Brown Bear Go?* by Nicki Weiss.
Have available a length of white butcher paper that can be used for a mural.

Focus: Ask the children to think of all the different ways an artist can make
a picture, for example, a pencil could be used. As children respond, list their
thoughts on the chalkboard. Review the list with the children. If they did
not mention crayon, colored pencil, collage, or watercolor, which will be
introduced in this unit, suggest those for the students to add to the list.

Objective: In order to introduce children to crayon or colored pencil
illustrations and to motivate children to create a crayon mural, share Nicki
Weiss's *Where Does the Brown Bear Go?* Show the illustration of the starry
night prior to the title page. Ask the children to closely examine the ground
and the tree in order to be able to suggest what medium they think the artist
used to make the illustration. As children respond, ask them to tell what
made them think of that medium. After children have responded, tell them
that Nicki Weiss used colored pencils to create the illustrations. Explain to
the class that the colored pencils of an artist produce a texture much like that
of their crayons.

Guided Activity: Ask the class to observe the illustrations carefully as the book is read. Urge the children to join in saying the repetitive lines. When the book is completed, discuss the location of the animals' home. If the animals had been real, which ones would have lived elsewhere?

Extending Activity: Suggest to the children that they bring a stuffed or toy animal from home that they could use as a model for a crayon-illustrated parade of animals on their way to school. Anticipate that some children may forget or not have an animal to bring for the next day's mural activity. If none are available in the classroom, borrow some from the media center or bring them from home. After the children have each made a crayon illustration of his or her animal on the butcher paper, a picture of the school may be sketched at the end of the mural.

FOLLOW-UP ACTIVITIES FOR TEACHER AND STUDENTS TO SHARE:

1. Before sharing *Hosie's Alphabet,* created by the Baskin family, tell the class that Leonard Baskin painted the pictures and his wife and children supplied the words. Ask the children to notice the water-color illustrations as the book is read. Go back through the book, having the children identify and use their own words to describe each animal. Let the children make watercolor pictures of an animal they would have included if their family were making an alphabet book.
2. Ask the children if they have ever wanted to be like someone else. Let them discuss specific traits they would desire. Tell them that, in Eric Carle's *The Mixed-Up Chameleon,* the chameleon wishes it could have characteristics of several zoo animals. Read the story. After completing the book, have the children look at the composite illustration of all the chameleon's wishes and talk about why the chameleon decided to be himself again. Let the children brainstorm body parts of other zoo animals that the chameleon might have wished for, such as the peacock's tail or the parrot's beak. Place on the chalkboard a large laminated outline or picture of a simple animal. Tell the class the animal is sad because he is so plain. Ask them to cut from construction paper an attractive part of one of the animals named in the brainstorming session. After all have made a collage piece, let each child name the part and tape it on the outline animal. When all the students have added to the collage picture, ask them if they think the animal is happy or attractive now. If they say "yes," leave the picture on display until the next day. Then read

Bernard Waber's *"You Look Ridiculous," Said the Rhinoceros to the Hippopotamus* (Houghton Mifflin, 1966). Again draw the children's attention to their collage animal. Do they still think he is happy or attractive? If they say "no," remove the parts. If they still feel he is better with the additions, put a sign or label below the picture saying "Our Mixed-Up _____."

3. Tell the children that, as *Jennie's Hat* by Ezra Jack Keats is read, they are to notice all the kinds of materials that appear to have been used to make the collage illustrations. After the story is read, ask the students to recall the materials that seemed to have been used, such as cloth, paper flowers, and valentines. Introduce the term "collage" and explain its meaning as an art work produced by fixing bits of paper, cloth, string, or other materials to a surface. Give each child an outlined paper hat. Using a variety of materials such as feathers, silk flowers, lace, ribbons, tissue, and fabric, let each student create a collage hat to be displayed on a "Jennie's Hat" bulletin board.

4. Tell the children that, as Leo Lionni's *Alexander & the Wind-Up Mouse* is read, they are to notice all the different materials used to create the collages. Share the book. Let the children discuss the materials they think Lionni used. Go back through the book, allowing children to point out materials they suggested and note any they failed to identify earlier. Give the children small pieces of gray construction paper and let them tear "Alexanders" to make a border for the bulletin board. Let the children use small pieces of black-and-white paper to cut or tear eyes to glue onto their paper mice.

5. Ask how many of the children know the story of "Goldilocks and the Three Bears." Have children describe Goldilocks and share in retelling the story in their own words. Tell them that James Marshall has used watercolors to make very humorous pictures for his book *Goldilocks and the Three Bears*. Tell the group that, as the story is read, they are to watch and listen for details in the text and illustrations that are different from the way they remember the story. After reading the book, let the children discuss the differences they heard and saw. Ask the children to recall some of their favorite Mother Goose rhymes. Repeat the rhymes together as children suggest them. Ask the children to pick a favorite rhyme and illustrate it in watercolors on paper. When the paintings are dry, label each with the appropriate rhyme and compile them into a *Mother Goose in Watercolors* book.

6. Share with the class Bettina Paterson's *My First Animals.* On each page cover the name of the animal with an index card and let the children identify each. After completing the book, re-examine the last illustration. Ask the children to look carefully at the picture and try to determine how it was made. If the children do not use the term "collage," which was introduced and experienced in Ezra Jack Keats's *Jennie's Hat,* repeat the term and review its meaning. Tell the children that, as the illustrations are shared again, they can decide how the pictures are different from the collage in *Jennie's Hat.* For example, Paterson uses only paper and, by overlapping and layering the shapes, creates depth in the animals. Explain to the children that, although the animals appear to be torn from paper, they are actually cut paper. Ask the children to think of an animal that is not in Bettina Paterson's book. Allow children to choose an appropriate color of construction paper and heavily draw the outline of their animal on the paper. Let the children tear or cut the animal shape they have drawn. Urge children to appropriately layer the animals' parts as Paterson did, using scraps of other colors as necessary. Let the children paste the finished animal on a sheet of white paper. Help them label their work with the possessive form of their names followed by the names of the animals, for example, "Gary's Giraffe" or "Paul's Snake." Make the pictures into an *Our Collage Animals* book.

7. Before reading Cynthia Rylant's *The Relatives Came,* tell the children that Stephen Gammell used colored pencils to make the illustrations. Ask the class to notice how the strokes of the pencil make them think they can almost feel the grass in the pictures. Read the story. Examine the illustrations with the class. Ask the children to speculate about why Stephen Gammell made all the strokes representing the grass go up and down rather than horizontally. Children should notice that the vertical strokes simulate the way grass actually grows. Using colored pencils or crayons, have each child draw a picture of what they might see along the road if they visited a relative in another state.

8. Before reading *This Year's Garden* by Cynthia Rylant, tell the class that Mary Szilagyi did the illustrations with colored pencils. However, the artist's colored pencils Szilagyi used are more like the children's crayons, with which the color can be applied heavily and scratched in places to produce more varied textures. Ask children to notice how the strokes help them visualize the texture of different objects in the pictures, such as carrot tops or dog's hair. Tell the

students that, when the story is over, they will be asked to recall a specific illustration they enjoyed. After reading the book, let the children talk about their favorite illustrations. Re-examine the illustrations, having the children point out areas of the pictures in which the colored pencil strokes are obvious. Draw attention to the close-up of the girl with her braids and straw hat. Point out how the repeating lines in the hat and her hair form patterns like the textures of the real items. Ask the students what favorite vegetable they would grow if they could plant a garden. Let each child use crayons or colored pencils to draw and color that vegetable. The completed vegetables can be cut out and placed in a paper cornucopia or basket on the bulletin board or in a real basket that can be displayed.

9. Before reading Nancy Tafuri's *Spots, Feathers, and Curly Tails,* ask the children to name farm animals and something about the appearance of each that makes it easy to identify. After the children have listed a number of animals and the unique characteristics of each, tell the group that Nancy Tafuri has used watercolors in her book to give clues by which they can guess each animal. Read the book to the class, letting the children guess the animals before turning the page to reveal each in its entirety.

Have the children suggest zoo animals and a special characteristic of each. List these on the board. Before children select a special animal to illustrate in their own class book patterned after Nancy Tafuri's work, explain to the children the watercolor method they will use. Re-examine Tafuri's illustration of the pigs. Notice that the color is darker in some areas than others. This mottled effect can be achieved by the method they are going to use. Tell them Tafuri used black pen for her outlines, but they will use crayons. Have each child make a large drawing of an animal in pencil. Then ask them to trace over the lines with a dark crayon. Before adding color, have children use clear water and a brush to carefully fill in the outline. Let children use the color of their choice and fill the wet brush well with watercolor. Lightly stroke the brush in the wet area, letting the color mingle and blend so that no brush stroke lines are seen and the entire area is filled with color. Demonstrate this technique to the children before they begin.

If desired, show the children the title page of Tafuri's book and point out that, if children are using two separate colors, they will need to complete one color and let it dry before using the second color. The second color will be added on a subsequent day. This will prevent the two from mingling together. After the children have completed their watercolor illustrations of the whole animal, they will need to make a watercolor on another page that shows a small portion of the animal and identifies its unique characteristic. When the pages are dry, add the text. Compile the pages so that each partial illustration immediately precedes the picture of the total animal. Let the children think of the animals they illustrated and decide on an appropriate title for their class book.

Chapter 2
Art: Second Grade/
Third Grade

Color and Value

OBJECTIVES:

1. Identify a monochromatic color scheme.
2. Comprehend shades and tints as the relative darkness or lightness (value) of a color.
3. Recognize that color and value repetition affect the mood of a work.
4. Show how color and value exist in the environment.

RECOMMENDED READINGS:

Dewey, Jennifer. *Can You Find Me? A Book About Animal Camouflage.*
Scholastic, 1989.
The title question inspires the reader to search the illustrations for animals
that use colors and shapes in the environment to survive. (Objective 4)
Fiday, Beverly and David. *Time to Go.* Illustrated by Thomas B. Allen.
Harcourt Brace Jovanovich, 1990.
Sombre illustrations in shades of brown reflect a boy's sadness on leaving
the farm and contrast with pictures of his happier memories of times past.
(Objective 3)

Hendershot, Judith. *In Coal Country.* Illustrated by Thomas B. Allen. Alfred A. Knopf, 1987.
Charcoal and pastels are used to illustrate the story of the joys and hardships of growing up in a coal mining town. (Objective 2)
Hort, Lenny. *The Boy Who Held Back the Sea.* Illustrated by Thomas Locker. Dial, 1987.
The use of color and value repetition lends emotion to the retelling of the old Dutch tale of the leak in the dike. (Objectives 2 and 3)
Lund, Doris Herold. *The Paint-Box Sea.* McGraw-Hill, 1973.
Both the various colors, shades, and tints in the illustrations and the figurative language of the text reflect the many moods of the ocean as observed by two children. (Objectives 2, 3, and 4)
McCloskey, Robert. *Blueberries for Sal.* Viking, 1948, 1976.
The use of blue for both illustrations and text heightens the effect of Sal's eventful day while berry picking with her mother. (Objective 1)
————. *Make Way for Ducklings.* Viking, 1941, 1969.
The story of a family of ducklings raised in Boston is told through monochromatic brown illustrations and text. (Objectives 1 and 2)
Ness, Evaline. *Sam, Bangs & Moonshine.* Holt, Rinehart and Winston, 1966.
Value repetition of shades of dull gold, gray, and aqua enhance the story of a lonely girl whose imagination causes trouble. (Objective 3)
Shulevitz, Uri. *Dawn.* Farrar, Straus and Giroux, 1974.
Subtle watercolors in blues and greens depict the approaching sunrise as it is experienced by an old man and his grandson. (Objectives 1 and 4)
Tafuri, Nancy. *Junglewalk.* Greenwillow, 1988.
Jungle scenes reveal many shades and tints of color in this textless story of a young boy's jungle dream. (Objectives 2 and 4)
Tresselt, Alvin. *Hide and Seek Fog.* Illustrated by Roger Duvoisin. Lothrop, Lee, & Shepard, 1965.
Color helps evoke the mood of life in a coastal village during a three-day fog. (Objective 3)

GROUP INTRODUCTORY ACTIVITY:

Preparation: Locate Uri Shulevitz's *Dawn.* Have paper, brushes, jars of clean water, and watercolors available for the follow-up activity.

Focus: Tell the children that they are going to hear *Dawn* by Uri Shulevitz. Ask the group if any of them have ever been awake to see the dawn. If any have, ask them to describe the colors of the sky just before dawn. If no one mentions shades of blue, show the class the first illustration in the book. Suggest to them that, as the story is read, they should notice that the illustrations continue to lighten just as the sky lightens as dawn approaches.

Objective: To satisfy the objectives of identifying a monochromatic color scheme and showing how color and value exist in the environment, read Shulevitz's *Dawn* to the class. Introduce the term "monochromatic color scheme" as a planned use of variations of a single color. Point out that black and white are neutrals and may be used in a monochromatic color scheme along with the basic color. Ask children to recall which portion of Shulevitz's book used illustrations in a monochromatic color scheme. Let children explore reasons why Shulevitz used the monochromatic blue only in the scenes before dawn. After they suggest reasons, reinforce the fact that after dawn the colors represent those actually seen in the environment.

Guided Activity: Re-examine the illustrations and ask children to find the first picture which they feel is no longer monochromatic. Most children will suggest that the illustration for "Now, a light breeze." incorporates green as well as blue, but their perceptions may vary.

Extending Activity: Have children examine the last illustration in the book which to Shulevitz represents sunrise. Have each student paint a watercolor picture of a sunset. Many children may want to use the technique learned in K-T-1 in which an area was painted with clear water, and color was allowed to flow from the brush into the wet area. Some children may want to allow each color to dry before applying another, as they did in the K-T-1 activity. Others may wish to experiment with adding one color after another, without the drying process, to allow blending between colors.

FOLLOW-UP ACTIVITIES FOR TEACHER AND STUDENTS TO SHARE:

1.   Before sharing Jennifer Dewey's *Can You Find Me?*, ask the children if they can explain the term camouflage in the subtitle. If no children can relate to the word, show the children a piece of camouflage fabric or clothing. Discuss why someone would wear clothing in such colors and patterns. Suggest to children that animals also use camouflage as a means of survival. As each page is read, ask a child to come up and point out the camouflaged animal. As a follow-up, ask each child to draw an animal that uses color as part of its camouflage. Have each student use crayons to create that animal's camouflage on a sheet of paper, then attach the animal drawing. Ask

students to label the animal represented on the bottom of the sheet. Tape a paper cover flap over each label and display the color patterns on a "Can You Find Me?" bulletin board where children may check their answers.

2. Introduce Beverly and David Fiday's *Time to Go* by asking children if any of them have ever moved to a new home. How did they feel about moving? Explain that this book is about a boy who is sad because he and his family, in hard times, are forced to leave their farm. Ask the class to listen closely and try to determine why the smaller illustrations on the right-hand pages seem happier than the larger pictures. After the book is completed, let the group discuss their ideas. They will probably conclude that the "happier" pictures illustrate the boy's memories. Re-examine the final illustration and read the accompanying text. Ask the children why they think the artist used brighter colors for this scene even though the boy was leaving. (The text indicates, "I'll be back someday.") As a follow-up, give the children brown paper grocery bags and ask them to tear a large rectangle from the sacks to represent the outer edges of one of Allen's illustrations. Have each child create a "Time to Go" picture of his or her own, using crayons or chalk in colors that reflect the individual's emotions about leaving. When the pictures are completed, let children place them on the wall in an appropriate section marked "Happy Leavings" and "Sad Leavings."

3. Show the children the title of Judith Hendershot's book, *In Coal Country*, and tell them that Thomas Allen used charcoal and pastels for the illustrations. See if any children can suggest why charcoal was selected as a medium. After reading the story to the class, examine some of the illustrations again to see how the use of the charcoal makes the reader feel that the coal dust is filling the air. Remind children that a shade is a darker value of a color that can be created by adding black to that color. Point out the use of charcoal to create darker values in the green grass in the illustrations of Mama with her washtub.

Give each child a large piece of white construction paper, pastels or colored chalk, and a piece of charcoal. Ask children to draw a thin rectangular strip down one side of the paper. Tell them to select a piece of chalk or a pastel and evenly color the entire strip. Instruct the children to leave the top of the strip the basic color. Have them use charcoal to shade the remaining portion, making it progressively darker until the bottom is as dark as possible. Explain that they have created a value chart showing the shades between the selected color and black. Encourage children to create a chalk or pastel and charcoal picture on the remaining portion of their page, using some of the shades shown on their value charts. Spray completed pages with hair spray or fixative.

4. Before reading Lenny Hort's *The Boy Who Held Back the Sea*, explain to the children that this is a story about a boy who saved his town from being flooded. Tell the class that illustrator Thomas Locker used a variety of colors to suggest the mood of scenes from the story. Ask the class how light colors make them feel and how dark colors make them feel. Record their responses on the chalkboard, being sure that they include emotional terms such as happy, sad, worried, or frightened. Suggest to the class that, as the story is read, they should look carefully at Thomas Locker's paintings to see how the illustrations help the reader know the boy's feelings as the events occur. After reading the story, turn back to the illustrations of the boy roasting a squirrel, the scene where the sunset has turned the sky orange, the spread of gathering storm clouds, and the full-page illustration of the boy's parents taking him home. Ask the children to choose either words from their list or new words to tell how each illustration makes them feel. Did the use of color and light and dark values affect their responses to the pictures? If, for example, Locker had shown clouds gathering in a light blue sky with bright sunshine, would the picture have given them the same fearful feelings as the dark storm clouds? Point out that use of dark shades of color gives a more solemn feeling than do light tints.

Tell the class that shades can be made from any color or medium, even a pencil. Give each child a sheet of paper on which has been duplicated a 1" x 9" rectangle divided into one square inch blocks with the extremes labeled "Lightest" and "Darkest." Instruct children to leave the "Lightest" block white and begin filling each block with pencil shading that grows consistently darker in each block until the last square is as black as possible. Ask children which end of the value scale Locker used to show the boy's fear. Which end of the scale was used when the parents carried him home?

5. Tell the children that many moods of the ocean are portrayed in Doris Lund's *The Paint-Box Sea*. Ask the class to suggest what color they would use to paint the ocean. Would they always choose the color they named or might the ocean look different on a sunny day, a stormy day, or a foggy day? After the children respond, tell them to

watch the illustrations carefully and listen for the descriptive language the author used to help them picture the colors in their minds. Stop after reading the page where Jane is painting the water red. Ask the children to recall the words used to describe the red color of the sea ("like tea" and "like a million goldfish"). Continue reading. After completing the book, ask the children to recall the colors and descriptive words the author used. Share again any pages for which the children could not recall the descriptive language.

Ask all the children to bring from home a small bottle or jar with a tight lid so that the next day they can each create an "Ocean in a Bottle." Pour the jar approximately half full of water. Let children use food coloring or ink to color the water in their bottle the tint or shade they desire. Add mineral spirits or a clear, lightweight oil to within ½" of the top of the jar. Cap the jar tightly. When the jar is shaken gently, the motion of the colored water and oil will produce a simulated wave. Ask each child to write a sentence using figurative language that describes what his or her ocean looks like. Tape the sentences on the jars and display.

6. Show students the cover of Robert McCloskey's *Blueberries for Sal.* Tell them that many of them have probably heard the story before. However, they will enjoy it again and they need to study the illustrations very carefully as the story is read. Tell the class that McCloskey used a monochromatic color scheme in his illustrations. Ask them what color they think he chose. After reading the book, examine the illustration of Sal walking behind the mother bear. Let the children discuss how McCloskey was able to present a mountain scene by using only one color. If the children do not call attention to the use of lines, solid color, and shape outlines to create contrast, point out these ideas to them. Ask the children to examine the text on that particular page and see if they find anything unusual about it. Be sure someone notes that the text is also printed in the same blue ink.

   As a follow-up, let each child share a canned, fresh, or frozen blueberry. Then ask the children to each write a paragraph about a favorite blue thing or about the value of berry picking. Have the children decorate their pages with an appropriate blue border. Urge them to incorporate blue objects into the design.

7. Tell the children that *Make Way for Ducklings* was inspired by Robert McCloskey's own experiences while living in Boston and attending art school. Later, while working on the book, he kept ducks

in his apartment so he could observe their actions, movements, and body details. Tell the class that the book won the Caldecott Award in 1942 and that it was done in monochromatic brown. Ask the class to speculate about why McCloskey chose a brown color scheme rather than another color. Tell the children that, as the book is read, they are to pay close attention to the body shapes and actions of the ducks. After reading the story, have the children discuss positions or actions of the ducks that they noticed. Ask the children to recall that McCloskey kept ducks in his apartment while working on the illustrations. Let the children discuss what problems might have arisen while he was trying to keep ducks in an apartment. Ask each student to draw a monochromatic brown illustration of some duck action McCloskey may have observed while the ducks lived with him.

8. Read *Sam, Bangs & Moonshine* by Evaline Ness to the class, holding the book so that the pictures can be displayed while the book is read. After completing the book, ask the children to identify the colors used. Note that Ness used shades (darker values of the colors) of gold, gray, and aqua to produce the illustrations. Let the children discuss how lighter and darker colors affect the way they feel. How do they think Ness wanted them to feel as they read the book? Did her color choices add to that feeling? Ask the children to recall a particular illustration in which they remember the shades being used very effectively to add to the mood of the story. How might the mood or feeling of the book be changed if Ness had used light yellow, pale blue, and pink instead of the colors chosen?

    As an extending activity play on a tape recorder or phonograph a piece of instrumental music with an obvious mood, such as Tchaikovsky's "Russian Dance" from *Nutcracker Suite* or Mussorgsky's "Night on Bald Mountain" (Walt Disney's *Fantasia*, Buena Vista Records, 1957, 8 s., 12 in., 33 rpm). Ask the children to listen to a few moments of the music and then choose two or three crayons that reflect the mood of that piece. While children listen to the remainder of the music, have them create an illustration that shows how the music makes them feel.

9. Before sharing *Junglewalk* by Nancy Tafuri, show the class the illustration of the boy reading *Jungles of the World.* Point out the areas of lighter and darker color on the boy's book or bedspread. Tell the class that lighter variations of a color are called tints and darker variations are called shades. These can be produced by adding white or black, respectively, to a color. A similar effect can be achieved by applying more or less of the color itself. Share the illustrations in the

book. While showing each page, ask a child to come forward and point out one example of a tint or shade. After completing the book, re-examine the illustrations by having the children tell the story from the pictures. Ask the children to suppose that the boy had been reading *A Day at the Farm* rather than *Jungles of the World.* Have each child paint a watercolor picture of a scene the boy may have dreamed after reading that book.

10. To introduce *Hide and Seek Fog* by Alvin Tresselt ask the children if they have ever been in a fog. What problems do fogs cause? If they were going to illustrate a fog, what colors would they use? Tell the class that Tresselt's book is about a three-day fog that envelops a small village on the Atlantic seacoast. Ask students to notice how the colors enhance the mood of the text and the figurative language it contains. Have them notice descriptive words Duvoisin illustrated in his paintings, such as "gray-wrapped rocks" and "empty gray-ness."

After the story is read, let the children recall figurative language they heard. List their responses on the board. If they omit some exceptional phrases like "fog twisted about the cottages like slow-motion smoke," go back and read those particular lines again. Now ask the students to select a phrase from the list of descriptive language and illustrate it by using crayons and adding fog to the finished picture with gray or white chalk. Spray each completed picture with hair spray or fixative to prevent smearing.

Shape and Space

OBJECTIVES:

1. Identify shape changes from realism to abstraction.
2. Recognize symmetry within a shape.
3. See depth by placement on a page.
4. Determine depth by amount of detail.

RECOMMENDED READINGS:

Cooney, Barbara. *Miss Rumphius.* Viking, 1982.
Symmetry and depth are evident in the illustrations of the Lupine Lady who planted seeds to make the world more beautiful. (Objectives 2, 3, and 4)

Cowcher, Helen. *Antarctica.* Farrar, Straus and Giroux, 1990.
Striking illustrations enhance the story of dangers that threaten the world of the penguins and seals. (Objectives 2, 3, and 4)

Crews, Donald. *Carousel.* Greenwillow, 1982.
As the carousel begins to turn, the graphic illustrations blur into abstraction and evidence motion. (Objective 1)

Hall, Donald. *Ox-Cart Man.* Illustrated by Barbara Cooney. Viking, 1979.
Detailed illustrations portray farm life in early nineteenth-century New England. (Objectives 2, 3, and 4)

Kasza, Keiko. *The Wolf's Chicken Stew.* G.P. Putnam's Sons, 1987.
Symmetry is present in many of the illustrations of the hungry wolf whose plans to fatten a chicken for his stew go awry. (Objective 2)

Lobel, Arnold. *On Market Street.* Illustrated by Anita Lobel. Greenwillow, 1981.
The shopkeepers on Market Street are designed from the products they sell and most illustrations display symmetry of form. (Objective 2)

Nixon, Joan Lowery. *If You Say So, Claude.* Illustrated by Lorinda Bryan Cauley. Frederick Warne, 1980.
Humorous illustrations include symmetry and depth in the portrayal of Shirley and Claude moving across Texas in their covered wagon. (Objectives 2, 3, and 4)

Spier, Peter. *Dreams.* Doubleday, 1986.
Abstract cloud forms take on more realistic shapes in the imaginations of the children viewing them. (Objective 1)

Yolen, Jane. *Owl Moon.* Illustrated by John Schoenherr. Philomel, 1987.
Soft watercolor illustrations enhance the story of a girl's first owling trip with her father. (Objectives 2, 3, and 4)

GROUP INTRODUCTORY ACTIVITY:

Preparation: Locate Donald Hall's *Ox-Cart Man.* Find several photographs of butterflies, some with wings extended, showing the symmetry between the wings, and some with wings folded so symmetry is not observable. Collect furniture brochures and copies of *House and Garden* or other home magazines for the follow-up activity. Label three large pieces of butcher paper, one with the heading "Symmetry," one with "Depth," and a third labeled "Symmetry and Depth." Either tear out pictures from the magazines or have a sufficient number of magazines for small committees to use.

Focus: Explain that symmetry occurs when an object is basically the same on each side of a dividing line. Display two of the butterfly photographs, one which shows the symmetry of the wings and one which does not. Ask the group to determine which of the butterfly photographs is symmetrical. Have a child use a piece of string to mark the mid-line of the symmetrical butterfly. Ask the children to compare the two sides divided by the string to determine if they are the same. Discuss why the second photograph is not symmetrical. Children should note that, because the photograph is a side view, both wings cannot be seen in their entirety.

Objective: To satisfy the objectives of recognizing symmetry within a shape, seeing depth by placement on a page, and determining depth by amount of detail, share Donald Hall's *Ox-Cart Man* with the class. Before reading the book, tell the class to examine Barbara Cooney's illustrations carefully as the book is read. They will be asked later to identify symmetry in specific illustrations.

Guided Activity: After completing the book, let the children re-examine each illustration and point out examples of symmetry. If no symmetry is observable, the teacher may want to call attention to that fact. In another session, share the illustrations in *Ox-Cart Man* again, explaining to the children that this time they will be looking for depth, the representation in an illustration of varying degrees of distance from the viewer. Remind them that in K-T-1 they learned that depth can be shown by the size of shapes and by overlapping. Tell the children that depth can also be shown by the amount of detail in an object and by placement of the object on a page.

Show children the first illustration in *Ox-Cart Man*. Draw children's attention to the large tree in the foreground, the trees along the lane, and those at the top of the hill. Point out to the children that the large tree is said to be in the "foreground" because in general the bottom of the picture represents the area closest to the viewer. The tree appears larger, and details of the bark and individual leaves can be noticed.

Now have the class look at the trees along the lane. Ask how the artist let them know those trees were farther away. Be sure they note the lack of details in the bark, leaves appearing in clusters instead of individually, the smaller size, and higher placement on the page. Call attention to the trees at the top of the hill. Ask children how they can tell that in the picture these are farthest away. Continue with the double-spread illustration of the farmer with the full cart and his family waving good-bye. Have children find examples of depth by placement on the page and amount of detail, e.g.,the ox compared to the animals on the hill and the trees in the foreground compared to the tree-filled hillside. Select two or three other pages which effectively show depth, such as the brick buildings and sidewalks at Portsmouth. Have children search for depth in the illustrations.

Extending Activity: Let each child select a picture from those previously prepared, or give magazines to small groups of children and allow each child to find a picture that shows symmetry, depth, or both. Allow students to share their selections with the group and explain which concept is illustrated. After sharing, each child can tape the picture to the appropriate sheet of labeled butcher paper.

FOLLOW-UP ACTIVITIES FOR TEACHER AND STUDENTS TO SHARE:

1. Introduce *Miss Rumphius* by telling children the book was written and illustrated by Barbara Cooney, the same artist who did the illustrations for Donald Hall's *Ox-Cart Man*. Explain to the children that, while the story is read, they will be looking for symmetry and depth in the illustrations. Share *Miss Rumphius* with the class. Then place the book in the reading corner. Assign children to small committees that will work together to examine the illustrations and find at least eight examples of symmetry and/or depth. Have each group compile a list of the examples found and the concepts illustrated. Perhaps multiple copies of Cooney's book may be obtained in paperback, from other schools if a system is involved, or through inter-library loan so that the entire class can do the activity simultaneously. When all have completed the assignment, the illustrations may be shown again and children can identify examples they selected in their groups.

2. Share Helen Cowcher's *Antarctica* with the class. After reading each page of text, let the children discuss the symmetry and/or depth evident on each page. After completing the factual text and examining the symmetrical illustrations, give the children black and white construction paper. Have each child make a symmetrical illustration of a penguin's full body or its face only. Let children affix their penguins to the bulletin board to create a collage rookery.

3. Before sharing the pictures and brief text in Donald Crews's *Carousel*, explain to the children that, as the book begins, the horses are riderless and standing still. Ask them to note how the illustrations change as the carousel begins to move. Cover the text and have the children examine the illustrations and describe the movement of the carousel horses. Ask the class to point out the illustration in which the carousel begins to slow down. How do the illustrations show the speed of the carousel? Point out that the blurred illustrations are a kind of abstract art. Show the children a large spinning top. Let them examine the top before it is set in motion. Then ask them to observe it as it spins. Have the children use their crayons to draw a realistic portrayal of the top they examined and an abstract picture of the spinning top in motion.

4. Tell the children that, as Keiko Kasza's *The Wolf's Chicken Stew* is read, they are to examine the illustrations for examples of symmetry. Share the story with the class. Then go back through the illustrations and allow children to point out symmetrical objects. Let them also identify objects that are almost symmetrical and discuss aspects that mar the symmetry, e.g., the chimney on the house and the wolf's tail in the illustration where the chicks are kissing him. Let the children use chocolate chips or nonpareils to decorate prepared cookie dough in a symmetrical design that the wolf could have made. Bake the cookies and let each child eat the cookie he or she prepared.

5. Read the introduction to Arnold Lobel's *On Market Street*. Tell the children that Anita Lobel's illustrations of the shopkeepers were made by using the products they sell. As the book is shared, ask the children to identify each product and the kind of store that would sell that item. After completing the book, suggest to the children that most of the illustrations are symmetrical, meaning that they are basically the same on each side of a dividing line. Re-examine the illustrations, asking children to identify symmetrical illustrations and point out what parts of some illustrations keep them from being symmetrical. As a follow-up activity, give the children paper clips, ice cream sticks, or other available objects that are uniform in size and shape. Ask each child to create a small symmetrical shopkeeper, using the items distributed. Glue each completed figure to a sheet of paper. Children may wish to use a pencil to add needed details.

6. Tell the children that, as *If You Say So, Claude* by Joan Lowery Nixon

is read, they are to look at Lorinda Bryan Cauley's illustrations for representations of symmetry and depth. Read the story to the class, then go back through the illustrations, having the children point out examples of symmetry (e.g., faces of characters and items of clothing) and/or depth (e.g., plants, rocks, and detailing on the snake). Let children create and decorate a symmetrical item of paper clothing for Shirley or Claude.

7. Introduce Peter Spier's *Dreams* by asking children if they have ever looked at clouds and imagined real objects in their shapes. Tell the children that the actual shapes of clouds are abstract, but the children's imaginations can place a more realistic shape upon them. Tell them that Peter Spier's book *Dreams* shows children who see figures in the clouds. Instruct the class to look carefully at the illustrations so they can follow the story because there is no text until near the end. Tell children that the double-spread illustrations are paired. The first double-spread shows the abstract cloud forms and the following illustration portrays the realistic forms the children imagined. After the class sees the illustration of the children lying in the grass, show the next illustration of them sitting up observing the clouds. Let the class imagine what the children see in Spier's drawing. Then turn the page to see what Spier portrayed. Continue in this manner with the students first seeing the illustrations of abstract clouds. Let them imagine what realistic forms can be placed upon the clouds. Turn the page to reveal Spier's interpretation. After completing the book, take the class to the school yard on a day when fluffy clouds are evident. Let children spend a short time examining the abstract shapes, pointing out to the class the objects they see. After returning to the classroom, have children tear from white paper a favorite abstract shape they saw. Have each child glue the "cloud" shape to the top of a sheet of contrasting paper and underneath draw the realistic form of that abstract shape.

8. Ask the children to listen for figurative language in the text as they view John Schoenherr's illustrations for Jane Yolen's *Owl Moon*. Help them listen by calling attention to examples early in the story, such as "The trees stood still as giant statues," and "my short, round shadow bumped after me." Ask the children to notice how the illustrations develop the idea expressed in the passages. Read the entire book to the class. Then ask the students to share examples of figurative language they heard. See if the children can find portions of the illustrations that develop the ideas in those passages. Ask the children to think about the illustrations in order to suggest how big

they believe the forest to be. Re-examine the illustrations, asking children to find examples of depth in the forest scenes. Children should identify if the depth is determined by the placement of the object on the page, by the amount of detail, or both. Call attention to the symmetry of the bird's body in the close-up illustration of the great horned owl.

Line and Texture

OBJECTIVES:

1. Understand that lines can give a sense of movement and direction.
2. Realize that lines can create the illusion of depth.
3. Recognize that lines can be used to create texture.
4. Examine the use of lines to create emotion or feeling.

RECOMMENDED READINGS:

dePaola, Tomie. *The Art Lesson.* G.P. Putnam's Sons, 1989.
A little boy is frustrated when he is not allowed to use his creativity in art. (Objective 3)

Emberley, Ed. *Ed Emberley's Great Thumbprint Drawing Book.* Little, Brown, 1977.
Emberley instructs the reader to combine thumbprints with simple lines to create a variety of characters that demonstrate emotions. (Objective 4)

Freeman, Don. *Beady Bear.* Viking, 1954.
Scratchboard illustrations use lines effectively in the story of a toy bear who could not be satisfied in the cave because something was missing. (Objectives 1, 2, and 3)

Leodhas, Sorche Nic. *Always Room for One More.* Illustrated by Nonny Hogrogian. Holt, Rinehart, and Winston, 1965.
Lines and crosshatching convey shape and depth in this retelling of an old Scottish folk song. (Objective 3)

Martin, Bill, Jr. and John Archambault. *Up and Down on the Merry-Go-Round.* Illustrated by Ted Rand. Henry Holt, 1988.
A sense of motion is enhanced by the use of lines in a simple story of riding on a carousel. (Objective 1)

McCloskey, Robert. *Time of Wonder*. Viking, 1957.
Lines are used effectively to create emotion and a sense of movement in the story of a hurricane on the islands of Penobscot Bay. (Objectives 1 and 4)

Parnell, Peter. *Quiet*. William Morrow, 1989.
Nature is portrayed through effective use of lines and simple text. (Objectives 1, 2, and 3)

Van Allsburg, Chris. *Two Bad Ants*. Houghton Mifflin, 1988.
In the story of two ants who face danger and return to the safety of home, lines are used to produce a variety of effects. (Objectives 1, 2, and 3)

Viorst, Judith. *Alexander and the Terrible, Horrible, No Good, Very Bad Day*. Illustrated by Ray Cruz. Atheneum, 1972.
The illustrations of a young boy's difficult day feature lines that show depth and texture. (Objectives 2 and 3)

GROUP INTRODUCTORY ACTIVITY:

Preparation: Locate *Two Bad Ants* by Chris Van Allsburg. Have drawing paper and pencils available for the follow-up activity.

Focus: Ask the children to define a line. After the group has formed a definition, have one student look up the word in the dictionary and share the formal definition with the class. Urge the children to think of uses for lines, e.g., lines on a football field, lines marking lanes on streets, and lines to mark maps. List student responses on the board.

Objective: After completing the list, tell the class that in *Two Bad Ants* Chris Van Allsburg used lines to show movement, direction, depth, and texture. Students may need to be reminded that texture refers to the way a material feels to the touch, e.g., rough, smooth, hard, or soft. Suggest to the class that lines in an illustration can imply texture. Encourage the children to watch the illustrations carefully as the book is read because they will be asked to point out ways Van Allsburg used lines.

Guided Activity: After reading the book, re-examine the illustrations. Let children point out pictures in which lines are used to show movement and direction, to give a sense of depth, or to create texture. After the students have discussed a number of illustrations, they may want to add these three new uses of lines to their list.

Extending Activity: Have students look around the room and choose a very small object that they will draw much larger, filling the entire page. Tell students to draw the outline of the object and then add lines inside the outline to show movement or direction, give depth, or create texture as Van Allsburg did in the illustrations for *Two Bad Ants.* Place the completed pictures on a bulletin board display.

FOLLOW-UP ACTIVITIES FOR TEACHER AND STUDENTS TO SHARE:

1. Tell the children that, in Tomie dePaola's book *The Art Lesson,* the texture in the hair of the children and adults is clearly shown by lines. Ask children to touch their own hair and think about how it feels. As the story is read, ask the children to find someone in the book whose hair seems to match the texture of their own. Have them notice how DePaola showed that particular texture. When the story is completed, ask the class why the little boy resented not getting to use his crayons to draw a picture of his choice. Allow the children to discuss their ideas. Let the children use crayons to draw a scene of their choice. Ask them to include a back view of themselves somewhere in the illustration, using lines to show the texture of their hair and clothing.

2. Introduce *Ed Emberley's Great Thumbprint Drawing Book* by drawing two curved line segments on the board, one representing a smile and one a frown. Ask the children if they know what emotions the lines represent. Let them discuss how they made that decision. Share the jacket or title page of Emberley's book. Tell children that the book shows how to add lines to a thumbprint in order to create characters and show emotions. Share pages 3–4 with the group, explaining that throughout the book Emberley shows what lines to draw and where to place them. Then share pages 7–8 in which Emberley demonstrates how one or more thumbprints plus a number of lines can be used to create a picture. Continue with pages 9–10 in which the author demonstrates how lines can be used to show emotion or feeling.

    Give each child four small pieces of paper. Pass a stamp pad around the room, allowing each child to make a thumbprint on each piece of paper. Instruct the children to write their names on their papers and place three of them in their desks to use later. Ask the children to pretend that the thumbprint on the remaining piece of paper is the head or body of an animal. Have them add simple lines to make the animal identifiable, e.g., the trunk and ears of an elephant or the mane of a lion. Ask the children to draw lines that will portray an emotion, such as happy, sad, or frightened. Tell children that the book will be placed in the reading corner so that they can examine it. They may want to use the remaining pieces of paper to create other characters. Label a bulletin board with various emotions. Ask the children to identify their animals, classify them by the emotions they show, and place them in the appropriate category on the board.

3. Introduce Don Freeman's *Beady Bear* by showing the students the black-and-white scratchboard illustrations in which lines are used effectively to depict movement, direction, texture, and depth. Read the story. Then re-examine the illustrations and have children point out examples of how lines are used. As a follow-up, ask the children to visualize an animal and think about how the animal's fur, scales, skin, or feathers would feel to the touch. Have the children draw the animal they visualized and use lines to show the texture of its body covering. Post the pictures on a bulletin board. Have the students think of adjectives to describe the animals' outer coverings, e.g., soft, smooth, or scaly. Let the students write the words on small slips of paper and affix them beside the appropriate pictures on the board.

4. Introduce *Always Room for One More* by Sorche Nic Leodhas by asking children to draw a picture of a person. After a few children have shared their drawings, ask the class if they can think of another way to draw a person. Show the illustration of the people dancing as the piper plays. Ask students to contrast their illustrations with that of Nonny Hogrogian. Children should note the absence of outlines in Hogrogian's figures. Tell the story as the children examine the illustrations. Have them note the texture of the cloth and the thatched roof as identified by lines. After completing the story, ask the children to draw another figure of a person by using Nonny Hogrogian's line technique.

5. Ask the students what they would include if they were going to draw a picture of a merry-go-round. After several students have responded, ask children how they could show that the carousel was moving. If no child suggests drawing lines, tell the children that lines can be added to show movement. Read *Up and Down on the Merry-Go-Round* by Bill Martin, Jr. and John Archambault. Now tell the children to take out pencil and paper. As excerpts from the text are shared, they are to draw lines or "doodle" to illustrate what is being read. Begin reading with "A prancing pig," and continue with pages in which the text suggests movement. After the reading is completed, have the children look at their lines and see if they can think of

specific words from the text that their lines portray, such as "up and down," "around and around," and "it's slowing down."

6. Before sharing Robert McCloskey's *Time of Wonder*, ask the children to watch the illustrations carefully so they will notice how the artist used lines to give a feeling of motion to parts of the pictures. They should also notice in which illustrations the lines help create particular emotions on the part of the reader. Read the story or tell it, being sure to show the pictures on each page. After the story is completed, go back to the illustration on pages 10–11. Ask the children to identify lines showing movement in different directions, e.g., the downward motion of the rain, circular wave motion created by raindrops hitting the surface, and the upward splash of drops. Turn to pages 14–15. Read the text about the growing ferns. Does the text add a sense of movement to the illustration? Now turn to the illustrations on pages 46–47. Have children point out lines that give a sense of movement on those pages. What emotion is created by the line? Other illustrations depicting a strong sense of movement or emotion through lines can be found on pages 20–21, 44–45, and 52–53.

7. In preparation for a walk outside, read Peter Parnell's *Quiet* to the class. Let the children examine the illustrations again to see how the artist portrayed nature. Draw attention to Parnell's use of lines to give depth and texture to the landscape and animals and to portray a sense of movement and direction in the waves. Take the group for a walk in the community, asking them to particularly note plants and animals they see. Upon returning to the classroom, ask students to each draw a picture of a scene they recall. Use lines to show movement, depth, or texture.

8. Tell the children that Judith Viorst's story *Alexander and the Terrible, Horrible, No Good, Very Bad Day* will be read just for fun. However, they should watch for examples of how Ray Cruz used lines in the illustrations to give a sense of depth or to create texture. Tell the children that, after they hear the story, they will re-examine the illustrations and have the opportunity to share their observations. After reading the story, the book may be placed under an opaque projector in order to make it easier for the whole class to see as each illustration is shared again. Let children point out examples of lines in the illustrations that create depth or texture. As a follow-up activity, give children scraps or swatches of cloth in a variety of textures. Have each child take one swatch and glue or tape it to the top of an 8½" x 11" page. Ask the children to draw pencil lines below the swatch to copy the cloth's texture as closely as possible.

Media and Methods

OBJECTIVES:

1. Recognize woodcuts in illustrations.
2. Identify pen and ink as a medium for illustration.
3. Be aware of acrylic and oil paints as mediums for picture book illustrations.
4. Examine scratchboard as a medium of illustration.
5. Realize the significance of the Caldecott Medal.

RECOMMENDED READINGS:

Berger, Barbara. *Grandfather Twilight.* Philomel, 1984.
Luminous acrylic illustrations develop the mood in this story of how each night a pearl becomes the moon. (Objective 3)
Brown, Marcia. *All Butterflies.* Charles Scribner's Sons, 1974.
Woodcuts illustrate this unusual ABC book in which letters are paired. (Objective 1)
————. *Once a Mouse.* Charles Scribner's Sons, 1961.
The grain of the wood lends texture to the woodcut pictures that illustrate this fable from ancient India. (Objectives 1 and 5)
Chaucer, Geoffrey. *Chanticleer and the Fox.* Adapted and illustrated by Barbara Cooney. Thomas Y. Crowell, 1958.
Barbara Cooney's scratchboard illustrations enhance the retelling of Chaucer's tale of a proud rooster who learns not to trust flattery. (Objectives 4 and 5)
Haley, Gail E. *A Story A Story.* Atheneum, 1970.
Award-winning woodcuts extend the retelling of the African folk tale about how Ananse brought stories to the earth. (Objectives 1 and 5)
Kennedy, Richard. *Song of the Horse.* Illustrated by Marcia Sewall. E.P. Dutton, 1981.
Black-and-white scratchboard illustrations portray the bond between horse and rider and the excitement they share. (Objective 4)
Krauss, Ruth. *A Hole Is to Dig.* Illustrated by Maurice Sendak. Harper & Row, 1952.
Pen and ink drawings illustrate definitions by young children. (Objective 2)

Kuskin, Karla. *Near the Window Tree.* Harper & Row, 1975.
Pen and ink line drawings and a description of why she wrote each poem make Karla Kuskin's poetry especially meaningful. (Objective 2)
Lesser, Rika. *Hansel and Gretel.* Illustrated by Paul O. Zelinsky. Dodd, Mead, 1984.
Vivid oil paintings bring the familiar Grimm tale to life. (Objectives 3 and 5)
Locker, Thomas. *The Mare on the Hill.* Dial, 1985.
Impressive oil paintings dramatize the story of a grandfather and his grandson helping a mare to trust people. (Objective 3)
Tejima, Keizaburo. *Fox's Dream.* Philomel, 1987.
Bold woodcuts illustrate the story of a fox seeking a companion. (Objective 1)

GROUP INTRODUCTORY ACTIVITY:

Preparation: Locate *Once a Mouse* by Marcia Brown, a small piece of strongly grained wood, several small pieces of very soft wood such as balsa, and one or more stamp pads.

Focus: Tell the children that as Marcia Brown's *Once a Mouse*, an old fable from India, is read, they are to notice the woodcut illustrations. Explain that woodcuts are a very old form of illustration. A book titled *Orbis Pictus* (meaning *The World Illustrated)* was translated into English in 1658 and used woodcuts to illustrate objects. To make a woodcut, areas that the artist does not want to print are cut away. The raised surface that remains is inked and pressed on paper to create the design.

Objective: To satisfy the objective of recognizing woodcut illustrations, tell children that there are three clues that may be used to help them identify this technique: large bold lines, sharp angles, and wood grain texture. However, not all may be visible in every illustration. Tell children that they can easily see all three of these visual clues in *Once a Mouse.* To meet the objective of realizing the significance of the Caldecott Medal, tell the children that this book won for Marcia Brown the Caldecott Medal in 1962. Share with the children that the medal is named in honor of Randolph Caldecott, an illustrator of children's books in the 1800s. The medal is presented each year to the illustrator of the most distinguished picture book for children published in the United States during the preceding year. The illustrator must be a citizen of or live in the United States in order to be eligible. If a reproduction of the medal is attached to the jacket or cover of the book, draw attention to it, pointing out that the picture on the medal is one that Randolph Caldecott created for his book about John Gilpin's ride. Read Marcia Brown's book to the group.

Guided Activity: Examine the illustrations again, letting children point out examples of bold lines, sharp angles, and wood grain texture. Can any of the children identify why Marcia Brown chose woodcuts as her medium for this book? If no one suggests that woodcuts were chosen because this is an old fable and woodcuts are an old art form, remind them that woodcuts are among the oldest forms of illustration, dating back as far as 1658 in *Orbis Pictus.*

Extending Activity: Share the piece of strongly grained wood with the class, drawing attention to the pattern in the wood. If the piece is small enough, ink the wood on the stamp pad and make a print of the wood grain for the children to observe. Give the children small pieces of balsa or other soft wood and allow them to etch a design in the wood with a blunt pencil or an old ball-point pen. When the children have completed their designs, pass one or more stamp pads around the room so children may make prints of the wood block designs. Encourage children to search for the grain in both the wood and the print.

FOLLOW-UP ACTIVITIES FOR TEACHER AND STUDENTS TO SHARE:

1. Introduce *Grandfather Twilight* by telling the children that Barbara Berger used acrylic paint as the medium for her illustrations. Explain that paint can be divided into two general types, translucent paints that have a transparent quality, such as watercolors, and paint that is opaque, such as tempera, acrylic, and oil paints. If a small tube of acrylic paint is available, it would be helpful to demonstrate the difference in the appearance of a brush stroke of acrylic and one of watercolor. Advise the children that several pages of Barbara Berger's story do not have any text so they must read the illustrations. Read the book, letting the children think through the story presented in the textless pages. Show the pictures again, asking volunteers to tell the story from the illustrations. After the children have finished telling the story, ask them to create in tempera their version of their favorite picture from the book.

2. Show the class the cover or title page of *All Butterflies* by Marcia Brown. Tell the children that this ABC book will be placed on the reading table, and during individual reading time they are to read the

book and examine the illustrations. After completing the book, they are to write a paragraph suggesting how the illustrations were made and defending their decision. Tell the class that each double-spread illustration has at least one butterfly in it. Some are hidden, so locating them is at times a challenge. (In "Ice-cold Jumpers" the butterfly shape is found in the aurora borealis at the upper right corner and in "Octopus Pants" there is a butterfly-shaped shell and three butterfly fish.) After all children have completed their paragraphs, have them discuss how they think the illustrations were made. Ask children to justify their decision. Let different children locate the butterflies on the pages.

3. Before sharing Barbara Cooney's adaptation of Chaucer's *Chanticleer and the Fox*, introduce the term scratchboard to the class. Ask the children to break down the compound word "scratchboard" into its root words and think about their meanings. Based on their knowledge of the root words, encourage children to speculate about what the term might mean. Children should be able to determine a close approximation to the actual process used in scratchboard art. After children have developed a definition, tell them that scratchboard is an art form which is often confused with woodcuts because the illustrations are similar in appearance. However, they are made in a very different manner. Tell the class that the term scratchboard describes the process as well as names it. To make a scratchboard illustration, black ink is usually painted over a smooth, white board. When the ink is dry, a sharp tool is used to scratch a picture on the black surface. The scratches reveal the white layer beneath and result in black-and-white illustrations. As *Chanticleer and the Fox* is read, ask the children to pay close attention to Barbara Cooney's illustrations because they won for her the Caldecott Medal in 1959. After completing the book, ask the children if they noticed anything about the illustrations that did not fit the definition of scratchboard. If no one mentions the addition of color, repeat the explanation of the scratchboard process, emphasizing the black-and-white results. After establishing the addition of color as the difference, tell children Barbara Cooney added color by using a transparent overlay. She could have chosen to add color by painting colors directly on the white surface before the black ink was added.

As a follow-up activity give each child a piece of white paper. Tell the students they are going to make a picture using a process similar to that used in scratchboard. Ask the class to choose one or more crayons and heavily color the entire page. Point out that the finished picture will reveal the colors they use, so they may want to think about the placement of the various colors on the page. After the page is thoroughly coated with crayon, allow each child to paint the entire page with black tempera paint to which has been added liquid dishwashing detergent in a ratio of approximately one part detergent to eight parts tempera. The addition of the detergent will enable the paint to adhere to the wax-based crayon. After the paint is dry, let each child use an ice cream stick, worn-out ball-point pen, sharpened dowel stick, or a dull pencil to scratch a picture into the black surface. The colors beneath will be revealed. After the pictures are completed, ask the children if the colors are all positioned where they wanted them to be. Suggest to the children that perhaps Cooney chose the overlay method of adding color so she could be assured that each color would be positioned exactly where she wanted it.

4. Show the children a piece of wood in which the grain is clearly visible. Point out the grain in the wood and tell the class that the woodcuts that illustrate *A Story A Story* by Gail E. Haley were cut and printed in the artist's own print shop. Tell the children that, as the story is read, they are to look for any wood grains visible in the illustrations that make it possible to identify the pictures as woodcuts. Tell the children that this book won for Gail E. Haley the Caldecott Medal in 1971. Ask the children to recall the significance of that award as presented in the introductory lesson on Marcia Brown's *Once a Mouse.* After the story is read, go back through the illustrations and, if needed, help children to locate the grain in the first illustration. Omit sharing pages where the wood grain is not clearly defined.

5. Introduce Richard Kennedy's *Song of the Horse* by telling the children that Marcia Sewall's scratchboard illustrations show the excitement the girl and her horse share as she rides. Let the children read the pictures to tell the story, asking them to note how the scratchboard lines give excitement to the pictures. Ask children to speculate about why Sewall put several pictures of the girl and her horse on the same pages. If they do not suggest that it gives a feeling of the speed with which the horse is moving, suggest that idea. After the children have told their version of the story, tell them the book will be on the reading table if they would like to read the story for themselves.

6. Introduce Ruth Krauss's *A Hole Is to Dig* by telling the children that the book includes definitions by young children and is illustrated in pen and ink by Maurice Sendak. Give each child a sheet of paper and

an ink pen. Ask each to draw a picture of a hat and write a definition below. Let children share their illustrations and definitions. Share Krauss's definition and Sendak's illustration with the class. How is Sendak's illustration different from their own? Children will probably note that the illustration is very detailed and children are wearing the hats. Children may want to classify the hats they drew by style or purpose. Read the words Krauss included without giving the definition or sharing the illustration. Ask the children to select one word to illustrate with pen and ink and define. Place *A Hole Is to Dig* on the reading table. After children have completed their illustrated definitions, they may want to compare them with Sendak's pictures.

7.   Introduce Karla Kuskin and her art by sharing the filmstrip *Poetry Explained by Karla Kuskin* (Weston Woods, 1980, 46 fr., col., 1 sound cassette). Now introduce Karla Kuskin's *Near the Window Tree* by telling the class that many poems in the book are accompanied by notes about why she wrote them. Almost all are accompanied by pen and ink drawings. Select the poem "Running Away" on page 33. Read the poem and Kuskin's description of the incident that inspired her to write it (page 32). Now ask the children to illustrate this poem with a pen and ink line drawing. Place the children's drawings on a "Running Away" bulletin board.

8.   Introduce Rika Lesser's retelling of *Hansel and Gretel* by showing the children the tapestry of the witch's house that hangs on the wall in the last double-spread illustration. Tell the group that the original was given to Zelinsky by his grandmother and it hung on his wall as a child. Point out that Zelinsky chose oils as the medium for his illustrations, and that medium allowed him to convey the darkness of the woods as well as the areas of glowing colors. If the book or jacket has a reproduction of a silver medal on it, tell the students that the book did not win the Caldecott Medal for Paul Zelinsky, but it was chosen as an honor book. Note that the honor medal is silver while the Caldecott Medal is gold. Read or tell the story, giving the children time to examine the vivid illustrations. As a follow-up, tell the children that oil paints are very expensive. Since they are not readily available, the children can use their creativity to make a gingerbread house instead. Use a cardboard box for the sides and create a basic roof from extra cardboard. Let the students cover the sides and roof with graham crackers. They may use a variety of small cookies and candies to make the second layer of roof, the windows, and the door. Decorate as desired. Place the finished product on

display. The following recipe may be used to "glue" the materials together.

FROSTING

3 egg whites, room temperature

1 lb. confectioner's sugar, sifted (about 4 3/4 cups)

1/2 t. cream of tartar

Combine all ingredients and beat with an electric mixer until frosting is very stiff (about 7–10 minutes). Keep frosting covered with a damp cloth at all times to prevent a hard crust from forming. This frosting will dry and become extremely hard in 6–8 hours. Makes 3 cups.

9. Before reading Thomas Locker's *The Mare on the Hill,* explain that the illustrations were done in oil paints. Ask the children to observe the art work carefully as the book is read. Tell the students to think about whether they would prefer line drawings rather than the paintings to extend the text. After completing the book, show the group the illustration of the boys preparing hay and oats on the snowy morning. Ask the children how the picture makes them feel. Would they have felt the same if the illustration had been done in another medium? Now show children an illustration from Locker's *Family Farm* (Dial, 1988) and another farm book such as Beverly and David Fiday's *Time to Go* (Harcourt Brace Jovanovich, 1990). Do not tell the students the authors, illustrators, or titles of the books. Ask children to look carefully at both illustrations and determine which one was done by Thomas Locker. Have children justify their decision.

10. Share Keizaburo Tejima's *Fox's Dream* with the class. Then, showing the title page of the book, ask the children what method of illustration Tejima used. Some member of the group will probably recognize the illustrations as woodcuts. Remind the children of the three clues to help identify woodcuts that were shared in the introductory lesson on Marcia Brown's *Once a Mouse:* bold lines, sharp angles, and wood grain texture. Call attention to the fact that the grain of the wood is not visible in Tejima's work. As a follow-up activity, give each child a clean styrofoam meat tray and tell the class that they will each make a print of their own, using a method somewhat similar to woodcuts. Ask each child to draw a picture lightly on the smooth bottom of the meat tray. Have the children go over their drawings with a blunt pencil to etch the lines deeply into

the styrofoam. Place a small amount of block printing ink on a tile or glass pan and spread it with a brayer. Allow children to roll the brayer lightly in the ink and then roll a thin coating of ink over the entire flat styrofoam surface. The styrofoam trays should then be pressed onto a sheet of art paper to create individual prints.

Chapter 3
Art: Fourth Grade/
Fifth Grade

Line and Texture

OBJECTIVES:

1. Understand that a concentration of lines produces emphasis.
2. Recognize that lines can be used to create optical illusions.
3. Distinguish realistic vs. abstract rendering of texture.

RECOMMENDED READINGS:

Anno, Mitsumasa. *Anno's Alphabet: An Adventure in Imagination.* Thomas Y. Crowell, 1974.
Many of the three-dimensional letters, painted to look like wood carvings, contain optical illusions which challenge the viewer. (Objective 2)
———. *Topsy-Turvies: Pictures to Stretch the Imagination.* Weatherhill, 1970.
Optical illusions abound in the illustrations of the curious little men engaged in activities that fool the eye. (Objective 2)
———. *Upside-Downers.* Philomel, 1988.
Illustrations with challenging optical illusions extend the tale of soldiers in the land of playing cards who quarrel about up and down until a wise king proclaims it is all in the point of view. (Objective 2)

Baker, Jeannie. *Where the Forest Meets the Sea.* Greenwillow, 1987.
Multi-media collages using natural materials enhance the ecological tale of an Australian boy and his father on a camping trip to a rain forest. (Objective 3)

Bunting, Eve. *The Man Who Could Call Down Owls.* Illustrated by Charles Mikolaycak. Macmillan, 1984.
Pencil lines create texture and emphasis in the drawings for the haunting story of the boy who carries on the owl-man's tradition. (Objectives 1 and 3)

Cobb, Vicki. *How to Really Fool Yourself.* Illustrated by Leslie Morrill. Lippincott, 1981.
Brief text and illustrations demonstrate how to create sensory illusions. (Objective 2)

Ehrlich, Amy. *The Snow Queen.* Illustrated by Susan Jeffers. Dial, 1982.
Delicate line drawings realistically portray texture in depicting the retelling of Andersen's moving tale. (Objectives 1 and 3)

Fleischman, Sid. *The Scarebird.* Illustrated by Peter Sis. Greenwillow, 1988.
Lines produce emphasis in Peter Sis's paintings of the lonely farmer who creates a scarecrow companion. (Objective 1)

Frost, Robert. *Stopping by Woods on a Snowy Evening.* Illustrated by Susan Jeffers. Dial, 1978.
Highly detailed line drawings augment the brief text of Frost's famous poem. (Objectives 1 and 3)

Gardner, Beau. *The Turn About, Think About, Look About Book.* Lothrop, Lee & Shepard, 1980.
Fourteen colorful abstract designs demand imaginative observation and divergent thinking when viewed from each of four sides. (Objective 2)

Grimm, Jacob. *Hansel and Gretel.* Illustrated by Paul Galdone. McGraw-Hill, 1982.
Full-color illustrations attract the reader's attention in this well-known tale of two children lost in the forest. (Objective 1)

Longfellow, Henry Wadsworth. *Hiawatha.* Illustrated by Susan Jeffers. Dial, 1983.
Fine-line pen drawings illustrate a section of the poem describing Hiawatha's boyhood. (Objectives 1 and 3)

Wildsmith, Brian. *ABC.* Franklin Watts, 1963.
Both abstract and more realistic renderings of texture are used in paintings whose subjects represent letters of the alphabet. (Objective 3)

GROUP INTRODUCTORY ACTIVITY:

Preparation: Locate *Anno's Alphabet* by Mitsumasa Anno. Have art paper and crayons available for the follow-up activity.

Focus: Introduce *Anno's Alphabet* by having children examine the illustration of the ax in the tree stump in the first portion of the book. Suggest to the children that this drawing is an optical illusion, which deceives the eye or presents situations that are inconsistent with reality. Ask the children if anyone can find an inconsistency in the illustration of the saw on the following page.

Objective: To satisfy the objective of recognizing that lines can be used to create optical illusions, share *Anno's Alphabet.*

Guided Activity: Have the children examine each of the double-spread pages, including each letter of the alphabet. Ask the class to point out the optical illusions where they exist. Discuss how Anno's lines create the effect. Have the children examine the border to see what objects indicative of the letter are represented.

Extending Activity: Suggest to the children that Anno's alphabet will be placed on the reading table. Have each child re-examine the book. Then ask each child to create, by using Anno's style, a wood-grained single digit number that contains an optical illusion. Instruct the students to prepare a border that contains groups of objects that illustrate their numbers.

FOLLOW-UP ACTIVITIES FOR TEACHER AND STUDENTS TO SHARE:

1. Ask children to recall their experience with Anno's optical illusions in the introductory activity. Point out that illustrators often use optical illusions to make the reader think about what is actually being seen. Tell the children that Mitsumasa Anno used optical illusions on each page of *Topsy-Turvies* to force the observers to stretch their imaginations. Share the textless book with the class, giving children time to observe the optical illusions on each double-page spread and point them out to the class.
2. Before reading Jeannie Baker's *Where the Forest Meets the Sea,* ask the children to watch the illustrations carefully as the story is read in order to identify all the materials from nature used in the relief collages. After the story is read, let the class recall the materials

observed. Ask the children to discuss why the artist chose real objects and the collage technique instead of watercolor to illustrate the story. Be sure students note that realism is intensified by the use of natural materials. Ask the class if the message of the story was rendered more effectively through collage than would have been possible with watercolors.

As an art activity, suggest that the children each make a collage using natural materials as well as classroom art materials. Give each child a paper bag and, as a class, take a walk during which children may collect bark, twigs, grasses, leaves, and other materials found on the ground that they wish to use. Let each child create a collage using the materials found.

3. Read Eve Bunting's *The Man Who Could Call Down Owls*. Review the illustrations, asking children to note the use of lines to create a realistic rendering of texture (such as in Con's trousers). Point out that this concentration of lines often produces emphasis, drawing the eye to a certain portion of the page (e.g., the striking feathered pattern of the owl). As a follow-up have the children study Mikolaycak's illustration of the feathers on the last page which describes the drawings and typography. Give each child a feather and ask them to use a pencil to draw the feather as accurately as possible. Instruct them to recreate the texture realistically and use a concentration of lines to create emphasis in one area of the feather.

4. To introduce the delicate line drawings of Susan Jeffers found in *The Snow Queen,* share the double-spread illustration on pages 30 and 31. Ask children to determine the center of interest to which the eye is drawn by the lines and colors in the picture. Although some may disagree, most children will select the child on the reindeer's back due to the bright red color, the direction of the lines in the shrubbery, and the position of the other girl who is waving goodbye. Because the story is long, tell it rather than read it to the class. Ask the children to study the illustrations as the story is told. Suggest that they note how Jeffers used lines to produce emphasis and help create the center of interest. After completing the story, go back through the illustrations. Let the class discuss how lines help focus the eye on the center of interest in each composition. Also ask the children to note how lines in the illustrations denote texture (the way something feels to the touch).

5. Introduce Beau Gardner's *The Turn About, Think About, Look About Book* by telling students that each design in the book can be interpreted in different ways. The identification of the design

depends upon the side from which it is viewed. These designs can be called optical illusions because the eye is deceived into interpreting the design differently as the page is turned. Share the first design and read Gardner's captions. Rotate the book so the design is viewed from four perspectives. As the remaining designs are shared and before the captions are read, ask the children to speculate on what each represents. As a follow-up activity, draw a tornado-like scribble on a large sheet of paper (see Figure 1). Rotate the paper and again allow the children to suggest what they think the design represents when viewed from each side.

Figure 1.

stocking cap

elephant's trunk   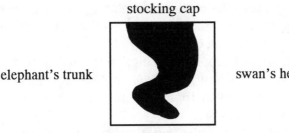   swan's head and neck

tornado

        Ask the children who wish to do so to draw and shade an original design, view it imaginatively, and write a caption (as Gardner did) for each side of the page.

6. Read Henry Wadsworth Longfellow's *Hiawatha*, excerpted from *The Song of Hiawatha* and illustrated by Susan Jeffers. Stop on each page to allow children to see the pictures and to note the use of lines in various ways to produce emphasis. Have the children notice the use of crosshatching (parallel lines crossing each other to produce emphasis or texture) on each page. As a follow-up, obtain a copy of Longfellow's complete poem *The Song of Hiawatha* from the library media center. Continue reading a portion of the poem from where the excerpt illustrated by Jeffers ends. As the poem is read, have the children listen and use colored pencils to draw their version of Hiawatha's forest.

7. Introduce Brian Wildsmith's *ABC* by telling the class that some of Wildsmith's paintings represent the texture of an object in an abstract rather than a realistic way. Share each illustration in the book and allow the class to discuss whether the representation of texture is abstract or realistic. It may be wise to begin by sharing the butterfly and the fish and suggest that these are abstract renderings of texture (one feels no sense of scales on the fish or of the soft smoothness of

the butterfly's wings). Compare those to the realistic interpretations of the nest and the yak (e.g., the smooth interior of the nest as opposed to the rough exterior and the coarse, matted hair of the yak). After all the illustrations have been shared and abstract vs. realistic rendering of texture is discussed by the students, tell the children the book will be placed in the classroom reading area where they may choose to do an individual activity as a follow-up.

FOLLOW-UP ACTIVITIES FOR INDIVIDUAL STUDENTS:

1. After sharing *Anno's Alphabet* in class, read the text in Mitsumasa Anno's *Upside-Downers*. Re-examine the illustrations from various angles. List and briefly describe five or more optical illusions. Indicate the page on which each can be found.

2. After sharing *Anno's Alphabet* in class, read pages one through seven in Vicki Cobb's *How to Really Fool Yourself.* Examine the suggested experiments and observations. Select one to demonstrate and describe for the class.

3. Read Sid Fleischman's *The Scarebird.* Re-examine Peter Sis's illustrations carefully. Choose three illustrations in which you feel the lines effectively produce emphasis. Describe each painting to justify your choice.

4. Read Robert Frost's *Stopping by Woods on a Snowy Evening,* illustrated by Susan Jeffers. Study the illustrations carefully, noticing how lines produce emphasis. Select three pages and describe what your eye sees first or is drawn to by the concentration of lines on the page.

5. Read Robert Frost's *Stopping by Woods on a Snowy Evening,* illustrated by Susan Jeffers. Study the illustrations carefully, noticing how lines produce emphasis. Go to the library media center and find another poem by Robert Frost. Select one or two lines from the poem and create a picture to illustrate the scene described. Use colored and lead pencils carefully to render texture and/or produce emphasis through a concentration of lines. Share your work with the class.

6. Read Jacob Grimm's *Hansel and Gretel,* illustrated by Paul Galdone. Study the illustrations, noticing how the concentration of lines in Gretel's hair and in the trees produces emphasis. Draw your version of the witch's house. Be sure that the concentration of lines in the roof or chimney add emphasis to your drawing. You may also use

lines to create other points of interest in your artwork.
7. After sharing Brian Wildsmith's *ABC* in class, choose a favorite illustration from the book. Reproduce the contour of the subject as accurately as possible, but use the opposite rendering of texture (e.g., if you feel that Wildsmith's rendering of texture is abstract, make the texture in your work as realistic as possible. If you feel the picture is realistic, make your illustration abstract.)

Style

OBJECTIVES:

1. Examine folk art, including Native American art.
2. View impressionism in illustrations.
3. Recognize cubism or abstraction as an art style.
4. Identify representational art.
5. Note surrealism in art and illustration.

RECOMMENDED READINGS:

Baker, Olaf. *Where the Buffaloes Begin.* Illustrated by Stephen Gammell. Frederick Warne, 1981.
Impressionistic illustrations heighten the mood of the Plains Indian legend of Little Wolf, who saw the buffaloes rise from the sacred lake and later saved his people. (Objective 2)
Drescher, Henrik. *Simon's Book.* Lothrop, Lee & Shepard, 1983.
Brilliant colors create a surreal world where pens and ink bottles come to life to help Simon escape from a monster. (Objective 5)
Glass, Andrew. *Jackson Makes His Move.* Frederick Warne, 1982.
An artist who is dissatisfied with his paintings discovers that abstract art allows him to paint his feelings. (Objective 3)
Goble, Paul. *The Girl Who Loved Wild Horses.* Bradbury, 1978.
Caldecott-winning illustrations reflect Native Americans' deep regard for nature in the story of the Plains Indian girl who becomes a wild horse. (Objective 1)

————. *Star Boy.* Bradbury, 1983.
Stylized drawings using Native American motifs lend authenticity to the retelling of the legend of how the Sun Dance was given to the Blackfeet. (Objective 1)

Howe, James. *I Wish I Were a Butterfly.* Illustrated by Ed Young. Harcourt Brace Jovanovich, 1987.
Impressionistic illustrations in soft pastels magnify the world of a discontented cricket. (Objective 2)

Locker, Thomas. *The Young Artist.* Dial, 1989.
Representational oil paintings extend the meaning and mood of the story of the young artist who refuses to compromise his artistic integrity. (Objective 4)

Raboff, Ernest. *Paul Klee.* Harper & Row, 1988.
Contemporary artist Paul Klee's work in cubism and abstraction is introduced through text and illustrations. (Objective 3)

Rylant, Cynthia. *Waiting to Waltz, a Childhood.* Illustrated by Stephen Gammell. Greenwillow, 1984.
Impressionistic pencil drawings recapture the past that is presented in thirty poems of the author's Appalachian childhood. (Objective 2)

Siebert, Diane. *Heartland.* Illustrated by Wendell Minor. Thomas Y. Crowell, 1989.
Representational paintings extend the poetry that describes the Heartland of America. (Objective 4)

Tompert, Ann. *Grandfather Tang's Story.* Illustrated by Robert Andrew Parker. Crown, 1990.
Grandfather uses tangrams to tell the shape-changing story of two fox fairies who played a dangerous game. (Objective 3)

Van Allsburg, Chris. *Jumanji.* Houghton Mifflin, 1981.
Soft pencil illustrations form a surrealistic world in which the children play the game "Jumanji." (Objective 5)

————. *The Mysteries of Harris Burdick.* Houghton Mifflin, 1984.
Fourteen black-and-white illustrations, each accompanied by a story title and first line, portray a surrealistic world. (Objective 5)

Wildsmith, Brian. *Brian Wildsmith's 1, 2, 3's.* Franklin Watts, 1965.
Simplified cubism is used to create illustrations of numbers in sequence. (Objective 3)

Zemach, Harve. *The Judge.* Illustrated by Margot Zemach. Farrar, Straus and Giroux, 1969.
Cornish folk art illustrations heighten the humor and reveal the conclusion of the story of the skeptical judge who pays a high price for his disbelief. (Objective 1)

Zemach, Harve and Margot. *Duffy and the Devil.* Farrar, Straus, and Giroux, 1973.
Lively folk art illustrations add humor to the Cornish variant of "Rumpelstiltskin." (Objective 1)

GROUP INTRODUCTORY ACTIVITY:

Preparation: Locate *Jackson Makes His Move* by Andrew Glass. Collect straws for each member of the class, art paper, and prepared tempera or watercolor paint in a variety of colors.

Focus: Show students the endpapers of the book. Tell them these represent Jackson's paintings. Ask children to describe the paintings and then discuss how the colors and swirls make them feel.

Objective: To satisfy the objective of recognizing abstraction as an art style, read *Jackson Makes His Move* by Andrew Glass.

Guided Activity: After reading the book, again share with students Jackson's self-portrait and the later one which Sloppy Joe thought was upside-down. Ask students to contrast the art styles of the two paintings. See if any class member knows a term that names either of the two styles. If not, introduce the terms "representational art" for the self-portrait and "abstract" for the second (because it attempts to evoke an emotional response rather than depict an identifiable subject). Which style did Jackson enjoy most? Can anyone suggest why? Reinforce for the children that some people prefer representational art while others like abstract art. It is a matter of personal taste and does not indicate the merit of each.

Extending Activity: Tell the children that each of them will do a form of abstract art by using straws. Give each child a sheet of art paper. Let each select three or four colors that reflect his or her feelings. Using one color at a time, have the children place a few drops of paint on their papers. Tell them to use the straws to blow the paint across the page. The students may repeat these actions, using each of the selected colors in turn until they are satisfied with their abstract work. After the paintings dry, post them around the room.

FOLLOW-UP ACTIVITIES FOR TEACHER AND STUDENTS TO SHARE:

1. To introduce the impressionistic style found in Stephen Gammell's illustrations for *Where the Buffaloes Begin* by Olaf Baker, show the children a photograph of a bison from a reference book or photograph file. Then show the class the double-page illustration of the buffaloes rising from the sacred lake. Ask children to compare and contrast the two illustrations. After the children present their ideas, introduce the term "impressionism" as a type of art and illustration that does not attempt to reproduce an object realistically. Rather, it gives an idea or impression of the object. Note that impressionistic illustrations often have a blurry or indistinct quality with many details omitted. This sometimes results from the artist's using closely placed short strokes or dots of color in the art work. Tell the story from the pictures, having the children examine the impressionistic illustrations as they listen. As a follow-up, have the children choose an object or animal and make an impressionistic watercolor of that object. Remind students that the impressionistic effect is often achieved by using closely placed dots or short strokes of color to create the object.

2. Introduce the term surrealism as an art style which is marked more by the subject of the illustrations than by the methods and techniques used. The surrealist presents detailed scenes which seem very real, but have a dream-like quality. Such scenes may contain unlikely combinations and incompatible images with qualities which are unbelievable in the real world. If possible, show the class a print of Rene Magritte's "The Return" (Shorewood Fine Art #1375, no date). Allow the children to discuss how Magritte's painting is inconsistent with reality. They should note that the songbird appears to be made of the daytime sky and a few children may realize that songbirds usually fly during the day, not at night as pictured. Read *Simon's Book* by Henrik Drescher, asking the class to examine the illustrations to notice surrealistic elements in the book. After completing the story, have the children recall illustrations which contain elements of surrealism. If necessary, re-examine the illustrations and assist the students in identifying surrealistic qualities, such as pens that writhe like snakes, Simon walking into the pages of the book, and the ink well creature. As a follow-up, have each child select an object in the classroom and create a surrealistic drawing of the object by combining it with a quality of an animal as Drescher did with the pens.

3. Introduce Paul Goble's *The Girl Who Loved Wild Horses* by calling attention to the stylized drawings found on the title page. Point out the characteristic two-dimensional quality of the art, noting that depth is conveyed by placement on the page and overlapping, but individual objects do not take advantage of shading to achieve a three-dimensional effect. Read or tell the story as the children examine the illustrations, noting aspects of the pictures that indicate the Native Americans' love of nature. After completing the story, turn to the double-spread page showing the two mounted hunters and the eagles flying above the girl and horse. Tell the students that Goble's illustrations are said to be stylized because they represent objects in a fixed pattern or design rather than according to nature.

   Have at hand information books or encyclopedias showing photographs of eagles and horses. Allow children to examine the photographs and look again at Goble's illustrations. Have them compare and contrast the photographs with the Native American art.

   Turn to the first illustration in the book, showing the girl on the horse framed against the sun. Discuss how the sun is stylistically portrayed. How would they draw the sun? What colors would they use?

   Read the Navaho song on the last page of the book, asking children to listen carefully to the figurative language found in each line. Reread the poem and let each child select a favorite line which he or she would like to illustrate in a stylized manner.

4. Read to the class the story of *The Young Artist* by Thomas Locker. Urge the students to study the representational art as the book is read. After completing the book, let the children discuss why Locker chose representational art to illustrate the story. After the discussion, tell the class that, in the time represented by the art, a court portrait served as a visual record much as a photograph would today. Have students compare Adrian's approach to painting with that of Jackson in *Jackson Makes His Move,* shared in the unit's introductory activity. As a follow-up divide the class into pairs and have each child draw a pencil portrait of his or her partner. Display the completed pieces on a "Who's Who?" bulletin board. Let the class examine the pictures and conclude whether the artists flattered their subjects.

5. To introduce *Grandfather Tang's Story* by Ann Tompert, show the children the last page of the book on which a tangram puzzle is explained. Tangrams can be used in storytelling by rearranging the individual pieces, called tans, into shapes that identify characters in the story. Tell the children that tangram puzzles are an example of

a simple form of cubism, an abstract art form wherein objects are broken down into the basic geometric shapes that form them. Tell the cumulative tale from Tompert's book, sharing Robert Parker's illustrations and the tangram shapes Grandfather formed.

As a follow-up divide the class into three groups and let each create their version of "The Gingerbread Boy." Give each child several sets of paper tangrams and have them create tangram animals which might threaten to gobble up the gingerbread boy. Let each group make a flip chart, gluing each tangram character on a separate page and placing them in the desired sequence. Let each group choose a narrator to introduce the story, allowing the other children to use the flip chart to tell the segment which includes the animal each created. After they practice the story, they may wish to tell a kindergarten or first-grade class about the use of tangram puzzles and share their storytelling efforts with them. Children may wish to get Paul Galdone's *The Gingerbread Boy* (Clarion, 1975) in order to review the plot of the story.

6. Introduce Chris Van Allsburg's *Jumanji* by telling the children that the surrealistic art in this book won the Caldecott Medal in 1982 for Van Allsburg. Let someone recall the importance of the medal. Tell the students that the illustrations are an example of surrealism because they present unlikely combinations and startling images or unbelievable qualities that may not exist in the real world. If available, share a print of a painting by Salvadore Dali or another surrealist to reinforce the concept. Read the book, asking children to look for surrealistic qualities in the illustrations and to be aware of the artist's technique of presenting the picture from an unusual angle or perspective. Re-examine the book, letting the children discuss the surrealistic qualities of the illustrations and the angle from which each scene is viewed.

7. Introduce *Brian Wildsmith's 1, 2, 3's* by telling the children that in this book Wildsmith uses a very simplified form of cubism. The artist takes simple objects and breaks them into their basic geometric shapes, maintaining recognizable forms. Inform the children that in each illustration Wildsmith formed a picture using a stated number of shapes. Tell the children to carefully examine the illustrations for the numbers 1 through 10. After the book is shared, the children will be asked if there were any pictures in which they had difficulty finding the specified number of parts. (In "10" it is difficult to discern which shapes to count.)

As a follow-up, show the children Wildsmith's illustrations of the ducks. Point out how the artist used cubist technique, distorting the true shape but giving the viewer a sense of the animals. Let the children use scraps of construction paper to cut geometric shapes and create a collage object.

8. Before sharing *Duffy and the Devil* by Harve and Margot Zemach, introduce the term folk art. Explain that folk art is a style that is characterized by the use of simplified and exaggerated forms to depict elements of a culture. Tell the class the story of *Duffy and the Devil*, sharing the illustrations as the story is told. Ask the children if this story reminds them of any other they have heard. See if any children recall "Rumpelstiltskin." Tell the children that this is the Cornish version of the tale. Point out Cornwall on a map showing the British Isles. Inform the children that Zemach's ink line and wash paintings are folk art. Share the illustrations again, pointing out the authentic dress and rustic humor representing the culture of Cornwall.

    Obtain Paul Zelinsky's *Rumpelstiltskin* (Dutton, 1986) from the library. Tell this German version as the children examine the illustrations. Let the children discuss the differences they see. In which story are the illustrations more humorous? Read the definition of folk art again. Do Zelinsky's illustrations in the second book qualify as folk art? If the children do not conclude that Zelinsky's illustrations are not folk art, reinforce the concept by telling them that these illustrations are realistic and do not use simplified forms and shapes.

9. After sharing Harve and Margot Zemach's *Duffy and the Devil*, read *The Judge* by the Zemachs. Share the illustrations as the book is read. Stop reading after the last page of text and ask each of the children to draw an illustration of the "horrible thing" the prisoners described. After the children have completed their drawings, share the remainder of the book. Ask the children if the illustrations remind them of any other book they have shared. After the class has had an opportunity to respond, show an illustration from *Duffy and the Devil* and ask if anyone remembers the name of the illustrator. See if anyone knows the name for the art style used in both books. If no one recalls the term, reintroduce the concept of folk art.

FOLLOW-UP ACTIVITIES FOR INDIVIDUAL STUDENTS:

1. After sharing Paul Goble's *The Girl Who Loved Wild Horses* in class, read Goble's *Star Boy*. Study the stylized illustrations. Examine the illustrations in *The Girl Who Loved Wild Horses* again. Write a paragraph describing similarities in the artist's work in both books.
2. After sharing *The Girl Who Loved Wild Horses* in class, read *Star Boy* by Paul Goble. Go to the media center and find an Indian legend that has not been illustrated. Choose a favorite scene from the legend and illustrate that scene, using Native American motifs similar to the style used by Goble. Write the name of the legend, the source, and a brief description of the illustrated scene on an index card and attach it to the back of the illustration.
3. After having shared *Where the Buffaloes Begin* in class, read James Howe's *I Wish I Were a Butterfly*. Recall that impressionistic painters attempt to give a feeling or idea of the subject rather than a realistic portrayal of it. This art style is often characterized by a blurry or indistinct quality that lacks detail. Write a paragraph in which you speculate about why Ed Young chose impressionism for the style of illustrations in this book rather than representational (realistic) art or photographs. Choose your favorite double-spread illustration from the book and explain why it appeals to you.
4. After having shared Stephen Gammell's impressionistic pencil drawings from *Where the Buffaloes Begin*, read Cynthia Rylant's *Waiting to Waltz, a Childhood*. Notice that Stephen Gammell captured the spirit of the past in Rylant's poetic memories of her childhood by using the same style of illustrations that he employed in *Where the Buffaloes Begin*. Recall an event from your past and make a pencil drawing to illustrate it. Write a paragraph or poem describing the scene.
5. After sharing *Brian Wildsmith's 1, 2, 3's* in class, read Ernest Raboff's *Paul Klee*. Klee worked in cubism and abstraction. List the names of the reproductions of his paintings that are done in the cubist style.
6. After experiencing *Brian Wildsmith's 1, 2, 3's* in class, read *Paul Klee* by Ernest Raboff. Using the medium of your choice, create a picture in the cubist style.
7. Read *Heartland* by Diane Siebert. Study the representational paintings which illustrate the book. Write a paragraph in which you speculate why Wendell Minor chose to illustrate the book with representational art rather than abstract.

8. After reading Diane Siebert's *Heartland,* go to the media center and find a poem that describes, in general, the type of community in which you live. Choose a verse or excerpt of the poem that you enjoy most. Copy the lines you selected and create a representational illustration that extends them.

9. After having shared Chris Van Allsburg's *Jumanji* in class, read the introduction to Van Allsburg's *The Mysteries of Harris Burdick.* Then read the title and first line that accompanies each surrealistic drawing. Select your favorite title and first line. Write a paragraph briefly describing the fantasy plot of the story you think would follow the line you chose. On another sheet of paper, write the final sentence for the story and make a surrealistic pencil drawing to illustrate that line.

10. After sharing *Jumanji,* go to the school media center or public library to see if you can find another book by Chris Van Allsburg. If so, read the book and examine the illustrations. Write a paragraph evaluating whether or not Van Allsburg used surrealistic illustrations in the book you chose. Share with the teacher a favorite illustration that justifies your response.

11. After sharing *Simon's Book* in class, create a montage, a type of collage made from pieces of other pictures. Select two or three old magazines from which you may cut pictures and arrange them to create a surreal montage by combining images that normally do not go together, such as an animal with a human head, a clock with human arms rather than hands, or an apple with a tree for a stem.

Artists Old and New

OBJECTIVES:

1. Realize how the artist's perspective affects viewer interpretation of a work.
2. Recognize the art of the old masters and modern children's illustrators.
3. Research the lives and works of the old masters.
4. Share how events in the lives of modern artists and illustrators affected their works.

RECOMMENDED READINGS:

Brown, Laurene Krasny and Marc. *Visiting the Art Museum.* E.P. Dutton, 1986.
A family visits a museum and notes examples of various art styles. (Objectives 2 and 3)

Fisher, Leonard Everett. *Ellis Island.* Holiday House, 1986.
Authentic photographs, original scratchboard drawings, and informative text highlight the history of the famous immigration station. (Objective 2)

————. *The Great Wall of China.* Macmillan, 1986.
A combination of black-and-white illustrations, calligraphy, and the red artist's chops (explained in the book) augments the brief text about the history of the Chinese landmark. (Objective 2)

Hyman, Trina Schart. *Self-Portrait: Trina Schart Hyman.* Addison-Wesley [distributed by Harper Collins], 1981.
Caldecott Medalist Trina Schart Hyman discusses and illustrates her life and art. (Objectives 2 and 4)

Keats, Ezra Jack. *John Henry: An American Legend.* Pantheon, 1965.
Marbleized paper provides striking backgrounds for several of the mixed-media illustrations in the story of the African American folk hero who died with his hammer in his hand. (Objectives 2 and 4)

Livingston, Myra Cohn. *Sky Songs.* Illustrated by Leonard Everett Fisher. Holiday House, 1984.
Acrylic paintings highlight the effect of 14 sky and weather poems. (Objective 2)

Once Upon a Time. G.P. Putnam's Sons, 1986.
A group of outstanding children's authors and illustrators have contributed anecdotes and art which share their excitement for books and reading. (Objectives 2 and 4)

Peet, Bill. *Bill Peet: An Autobiography.* Houghton Mifflin, 1989.
New drawings and illustrations from other Peet works enhance the story of the author-illustrator's life. (Objectives 2 and 4)

Raboff, Ernest. *Diego Rodriguez de Silva y Velasquez.* Harper & Row, 1988.
Brief text, accompanying thirty color reproductions of paintings, offers a critical interpretation of the work of Velasquez. (Objectives 2 and 3)

————. *Henri Rousseau.* Harper & Row, 1988.
Brief text offers critical interpretations of fifteen color reproductions of Rousseau's works. (Objectives 2 and 3)

————. *Pablo Picasso.* Harper & Row, 1987.

Through text and reproductions of Picasso's art the reader may gain insight into his life and art style. (Objectives 2, 3, and 4)

————. *Vincent Van Gogh.* Harper, 1988.

Quotes from the artist enhance the viewer's ability to interpret the reproductions of important works by Van Gogh. (Objectives 2, 3, and 4)

Rylant, Cynthia. *All I See.* Illustrated by Peter Catalanotto. Orchard, 1988.

By observing an artist at work, a small boy learns to see with the eyes of an artist and to share his vision of the world with others. (Objective 1)

Sills, Leslie. *Inspirations: Stories about Women Artists.* Albert Whitman, 1989.

Presents the lives and art of four modern female artists: Georgia O'Keefe, Frida Kahlo, Alice Neel, and Faith Ringgold. (Objectives 2 and 4)

Sing a Song of Popcorn. Illustrated by nine Caldecott Medal artists. Scholastic, 1988.

Nine Caldecott medalists demonstrate a variety of styles as they illustrate 128 poems. (Objective 2)

Stevenson, James. *Higher on the Door.* Greenwillow, 1987.

In a sequel to *When I Was Nine,* Stevenson remembers growing up in a small town in the 1930s. (Objectives 2 and 4)

————. *When I Was Nine.* Greenwillow, 1986.

Stevenson illustrates and briefly reminisces about his family life when he was nine. (Objectives 2 and 4)

Van Allsburg, Chris. *The Polar Express.* Houghton Mifflin, 1985.

Dark, rich colors add mystery to the illustrations of the boy who journeys to the North Pole and receives the first gift of Christmas from Santa Claus. (Objective 1)

Wood, Audrey. *The Napping House.* Illustrated by Don Wood. Harcourt Brace Jovanovich, 1984.

The perspective of the illustrations changes in this cumulative tale describing how a flea disrupts a sleeping household. (Objective 1)

GROUP INTRODUCTORY ACTIVITY:

Preparation: Locate Myra Cohn Livingston's *Sky Songs,* illustrated by Leonard Everett Fisher, and Leonard Everett Fisher's *Ellis Island.*

Focus: Introduce Leonard Everett Fisher by telling the class that he has written and/or illustrated more than 250 books. He received the Pulitzer Prize for painting in 1950. Explain that the Pulitzer Prize is an annual award given for excellence in areas of the arts and journalism. Tell the class that Leonard Fisher works in a variety of media. The art in the book the children will share was created with acrylic paint in the same size as it appears in the book.

Objective: To satisfy the objective of recognizing the art of modern children's illustrators, share Leonard Everett Fisher's illustrations for Myra Cohn Livingston's *Sky Songs.* Show the double-spread illustration for "Storm" and read Livingston's poem. Let the children discuss how Fisher's illustration extends the figurative language of the poem.

Guided Activity: Read the poem "Noon" without sharing the illustration. Ask the children to speculate about the colors they think Fisher used for his painting of that poem. Share the illustration. Read "Rain," letting the children speculate on the content of Fisher's illustrations and the colors used. Share the illustration so students can confirm or reassess their earlier conjectures.

Extending Activity: Show the class the illustration of "Storm" as the poem is read again. Ask the children to extend the painting downward to the ground in their minds, visualizing the figurative language Livingston used. Have children use colored chalk or another medium to prepare an illustration that seems to extend Fisher's painting downward.

On the following day share Fisher's scratchboard illustrations on pages 13, 24–25, 43, and 57 of *Ellis Island.* Read the excerpt in the text that each illustration extends. Let children recall how scratchboard illustrations are made (see the Media and Methods unit, chapter 2). Ask them to explore why scratchboard rather than acrylic paint was an appropriate medium for his original illustrations in this book. Be sure children realize that the black-and-white scratchboards harmonize with the black-and-white photographs used. Ask the children to speculate why Fisher chose to write and illustrate this book. After they have shared their ideas, tell the children that Fisher's mother came through Ellis Island in 1906 when she was six years old. Suggest to the children that some of them may want to read the entire book and research in the media center about the reopening of Ellis Island to visitors in 1990 after lengthy restoration.

FOLLOW-UP ACTIVITIES FOR TEACHER AND STUDENTS TO SHARE:

1. Introduce Laurene and Marc Brown's *Visiting the Art Museum* by asking what the children's reaction would be if a parent said the family was going to visit the art museum. After the children respond,

show the first double-spread illustration on the back of the title page and have the class discuss the boy's reaction. Tell the class the book will be placed on the library table or in a learning center so that each child can read it. Ask them to follow the boy's reactions to the art and see if his attitude changes by the end of the book.

All art work is identified in the back of the book. Ask each child to select one of the art pieces represented by Marc Brown for further research. Using the school or public library, each child should try to find a reproduction of the illustration chosen or another work by that artist to share with the class.

Instruct the children to choose any art work and visualize it as a "stop-action" scene from a movie or video. Ask them to write a paragraph predicting what would happen next if the scene in that art work continued. If they prefer, they can draw the picture rather than write a paragraph.

2. Introduce Ezra Jack Keats by letting the children view *Ezra Jack Keats* (Weston Woods, n.d., 17 min.). After viewing the videotape, have the class discuss information they learned about Ezra Jack Keats and where he got his ideas for his books. Show the children the first double-spread illustration in Keats's book *John Henry: An American Legend*. Ask the children how they think Ezra Jack Keats made the background illustrations. As the story is read, suggest that the children notice other backgrounds or portions of illustrations that may have been made in the same manner.

As a follow-up activity after sharing the story, have the children make marbleized paper. Use Helen Sattler's directions on pages 105–106 in *Recipes for Art and Craft Materials* (Lothrop, Lee & Shepard, 1987) as a guide. If a simpler method is desired, a similar but less effective look can be achieved by shaving colored chalk into powder which can be floated on top of water. Swirl the powdered chalk into the desired design and lay a sheet of paper gently on the surface. Lift the paper and set aside to dry. Spray the dried paper with fixative to set the chalk.

3. Introduce *Once Upon a Time* by telling the class that many well-known authors and illustrators represented in the collection have shared memories of their early life and their love of reading or drawing. Share Trina Schart Hyman's illustration on page 32 and read her short excerpt "Little Red Riding Hood" on page 33. Let the children discuss factors in Hyman's early life that contributed to her choice of a career in illustrating for children. As a follow-up, ask the

children to select one of the other artists in the book. Read that person's selection, and write a paragraph describing how the artist's work has been affected by an event in his or her early life.

4. Read the first two pages of Ernest Raboff's *Pablo Picasso*. Encourage discussion of the meaning of selected Picasso quotes. Share the descriptions of "Bowl of Fruit and Loaves on a Table" and "Three Musicians." After viewing the reproductions and listening to the text, remind the children that Picasso worked in many different styles, but cubism is one for which he is noted. As a follow-up, urge the children to read the book and complete the individual activity relating to it.

5. Before sharing *Vincent Van Gogh* by Ernest Raboff, explain to the children that Van Gogh was one of the first impressionistic painters. Remind them that impressionism is an art style in which the artist uses short strokes of different colors to give an impression or idea of an object as it appears in nature. Read the text and allow children to examine the reproductions of Van Gogh's works. While children are studying the reproduction of "The Starry Night," point out the short strokes of color that are characteristic of impressionism. Tell children that, if they had the opportunity to view the original painting at the Museum of Modern Art in New York City, they would need to view it from a distance. When viewed at close range, the short curved strokes stand out individually and detract from the painting as a whole. Note that this does not happen when viewing the reproductions because they are duplicated in a smaller, more compact size.

   After sharing the book, ask the children if they can recall the title or content of any particular Van Gogh painting they especially enjoyed. Re-examine the paintings the children identify and allow the class to comment upon why they enjoyed the particular piece.

   As a follow-up, allow a committee of children to go to the media center to find a reproduction of some other Van Gogh work, such as "Sunflowers." The one they locate may be shared with the class.

6. Read Cynthia Rylant's *All I See* to the class while, in the background, softly playing Ludwig van Beethoven's *Symphony No. 5 in C, Opus 67* (Columbia MG-3037, n.d., 4s, 12 in., 33 rpm). After completing the book, have students list all the synonyms for "see" that they can recall and identify specific meanings of each. Ask the students to determine which word best describes the boy's ability to observe. What was the difference between the way in which the boy and the artist viewed the world?

As a follow-up have the children go outside and carefully study a scene they would like to paint. Suggest they take a sketchpad along to sketch the scene so it can jog their memories later. Have students paint their scenes while listening to a musical selection appropriate to the setting. For example, in an urban setting George Gershwin's "Concerto for Piano and Orchestra in F" or "American in Paris" (RCA VCS7097, n.d., 4s, 12 in., 33 rpm) might be selected. Beethoven's *Symphony No. 6 in F, Opus 68* "Pastoral" (ANG D38286, n.d., 12 in., 33 rpm) might be more appropriate for rural settings. Display the children's finished products in a school or class art gallery.

7. Tell the children that *Sing a Song of Popcorn* is a collection of poems illustrated by nine well-known illustrators who have each received the Caldecott Medal. Show the children the illustrations for "The Jumblies" on pages 51–55. Let the students speculate on the identity of the artist who did the illustrations. Have them justify the suggestions they made. Then read the poem "The Jumblies," allowing the children to examine the illustrations further as the poem is read. After concluding the poem, see if there are other suggestions about the artist's identity. Poll the class to see if a consensus can be reached.

   Tell the class that Maurice Sendak did the illustrations for the poem. Share the illustrations from *Where the Wild Things Are* (Harper & Row, 1963) or *Chicken Soup with Rice* (Harper & Row, 1962). Ask the children if they can see any similarities in the styles used in both works. Ask each child to go to the media center and find a poem he or she likes that is not included in *Sing a Song of Popcorn*. Ask each to decide which of the nine artists from *Sing a Song of Popcorn* the student would choose to illustrate the selected poem. Instruct each child to copy four lines that best represent the mood of the poem. Have each write a brief paragraph justifying the choice of an illustrator.

8. Introduce *Inspirations: Stories about Women Artists* by Leslie Sills. Tell the children that four modern artists are included in the book, but they will hear about Georgia O'Keefe (pages 6–17). Ask the class to listen for events in her life that they feel affected her painting. After reading the section, let the children re-examine the reproductions of her art and discuss events that influenced the painting of each.

9. Read James Stevenson's *When I Was Nine* to the group. Ask the children to discuss why certain events he describes were memorable for Stevenson. As a follow-up, allow each child to make a watercolor

picture of a memorable event that happened to him or her in the past year. Have each child label the event and display the finished products in the classroom.

10. Introduce Audrey Wood's *The Napping House* by telling the children that this book is an excellent example of perspective. Review the term perspective as referring to the reference point of the artist or viewer relative to the position and distance of the objects in the artwork. Tell the children that, as *The Napping House* is read, they are to watch the illustrations, particularly the chair and the bed. Ask them to notice changes in perspective as the story unfolds. After completing the story, let children discuss the changing perspective they found. Children should observe that the angle of viewing gradually increases until the viewer looks almost directly down from above the bed. Then the viewing angle gradually decreases to the original perspective. If students have difficulty seeing the shifts in perspective, ask them to concentrate on the chair in each picture and follow the changes through that one object.

Note the picture of the house at the first of the story. Ask children to visualize where they would be located if they, the viewers, were extensions of the scene. If children are unable to place their locations, point out that they seem to be above the porch (because they can see the porch roof) but below the roof of the house (because they can see only the edge and underside of the eaves). Ask children to find other objects in the painting that demonstrate perspective. As a follow-up, ask each child to choose a simple object from the classroom and draw it from three different perspectives.

FOLLOW-UP ACTIVITIES FOR INDIVIDUAL STUDENTS:

1. After reading *The Great Wall of China* by Leonard Everett Fisher, read the information about "chops" on the back of the title page. Design a chop that you feel represents you. It may or may not include your name or initials. Use your chop to sign an original illustration you create.

2. After sharing *Once Upon a Time* in class, read Trina Schart Hyman's *Self-Portrait*. Identify ten events in her life that affected her art or caused her to illustrate particular books. As an alternative activity you may go to the media center and find a book Hyman has illustrated. List similarities in Hyman's style in both books.

3. Read *Bill Peet: An Autobiography*. Share a brief biographical sketch of the author-illustrator with the class. Be sure to include events in his life that affected his work. As an alternative activity you may go to the media center and find a book by Bill Peet that is mentioned in his autobiography. Share a picture from that book with the class and tell why Bill Peet chose to write and illustrate that particular book.

4. Read Ernest Raboff's *Diego Rodriguez de Silva y Velasquez*. In the time of Velasquez modern photography had not been developed and portraits were the only visual record of people's appearance. Velasquez was a master of the portrait. Study his use of detail in the reproductions of his portraits that make his subjects lifelike. Using the medium of your choice create a portrait of a member of your family. Be as accurate as possible. Share the results with the class and discuss the degree of difficulty found in portrait art.

5. Read Ernest Raboff's *Henri Rousseau*. Rousseau has been called "The Master of the Trees." After reading the book, study the trees in the illustrations. Write a paragraph suggesting why you think he was given that title.

6. After sharing part of Ernest Raboff's *Pablo Picasso* in class, read the entire work and answer the following questions:
   a. Why did Picasso paint many pictures of circus people?
   b. In addition to painting, Picasso is noted for his work in what other art form?
   c. In the final sentence of the book Picasso is identified as a "painter, historian, sculptor, father, poet, scholar, husband." Choose any two of those nouns and pair them with at least two descriptive words (adjectives). Use each pair of words in an original sentence relating to Picasso.
   d. After reading the book, re-examine the art reproductions and choose the work you like most and the work you like least. Identify each and explain what elements of each work cause your reaction to them.

7. After sharing in class the chapter on the life and work of Georgia O'Keefe from *Inspirations: Stories about Women Artists* by Leslie Sills, choose one of the three remaining artists and read the chapter about her from the book. Make a list of what you feel to be the ten most important influences on her art. The teacher may ask you to share your opinion with the class.

8. After sharing James Stevenson's *When I Was Nine* in class, read his book *Higher on the Door*. Examine again the illustration of things Stevenson was afraid of. Make a watercolor illustration of something that frightens you.

9. Read James Stevenson's *Higher on the Door*. Stevenson concludes his book with, "I couldn't wait to get higher on the door." Create a watercolor illustration of what you hope to do when you are "higher on the door."

10. Read Chris Van Allsburg's *The Polar Express*. Go through the illustrations and choose the one which you feel shows the most unusual artist's perspective. Write a paragraph justifying your choice and describing where you would be located relative to the action in the illustration if you, the viewer, were an extension of the scene.

Media and Methods

OBJECTIVES:

1. Explore photography as a medium for illustration.
2. Recognize pen and pencil drawing as a medium for illustration.
3. Study illustrated representations of three-dimensional art.
4. Realize how paper folding and cutting can be used as an art form.
5. Compare the art used to portray variations of the same story.

RECOMMENDED READINGS:

Arnosky, Jim. *Sketching Outdoors in Autumn*. Lothrop, Lee & Shepard, 1988.
   In addition to a descriptive text, Arnosky gives italicized directions for creating detailed line drawings. (Objective 2)
Bang, Molly. *The Paper Crane*. Greenwillow, 1985.
   A crane folded from a paper napkin comes to life, attracting customers to an out-of-the-way restaurant by its magical dancing. (Objective 4)
Baylor, Byrd. *When Clay Sings*. Illustrated by Tom Bahti. Charles Scribner's Sons, 1972.
   Poetic text pays tribute to the prehistoric Native American pottery makers of the desert southwest. (Objective 3)

Brett, Jan. *Beauty and the Beast.* Clarion, 1989.
Elaborate illustrations depict the beast as a wild boar in this brief retelling of the classic tale. (Objective 5)

Fleischman, Paul. *The Animal Hedge.* Illustrated by Lydia Dabcovich. E.P. Dutton, 1983.
Through sculpting a hedge, a farmer recreates his past, and his sons find their destinies. (Objective 3)

Froman, Robert. *Seeing Things: A Book of Poems.* Lettering by Ray Barber. Thomas Y. Crowell, 1974.
Appropriate lettering and line drawings illustrate the subjects of the 51 poems included. (Objective 2)

Grimm, Jacob. *Snow White.* Illustrated by Trina Schart Hyman. Little, Brown, 1974.
Lush paintings depict this edition of the German folk tale. (Objective 5)

————. *Snow-White and the Seven Dwarfs.* Illustrated by Nancy Ekholm Burkert. Farrar, Straus, & Giroux, 1972.
Meticulous research provided background for the intricate double-spread illustrations in this version translated by Randall Jarrell. (Objective 5)

Hoban, Tana. *Shadows and Reflections.* Greenwillow, 1990.
Striking color photographs illuminate the concepts of shadows and reflections. (Objective 1)

Irvine, Joan. *How to Make Pop-Ups.* Illustrated by Barbara Reid. Morrow, 1987.
Activities for paper cutting as an art craft are explained and illustrated. (Objective 4)

Krementz, Jill. *A Very Young Gymnast.* Alfred A. Knopf, 1978.
Black-and-white photographs capture the spirit, dedication, and excitement of a ten-year-old gymnast as she practices and competes. (Objective 1)

Lasky, Kathryn. *Dinosaur Dig.* Illustrated by Christopher G. Knight. William Morrow, 1990.
Color photographs record a family's trip to participate in a paleontology dig. (Objective 1)

Lauber, Kathryn. *Volcano: The Eruption and Healing of Mount St. Helens.* Bradbury, 1986.
Color photographs dramatize the account of the eruption of Mount St. Helens and the recovery of the area. (Objective 1)

Mayer, Marianna. *Beauty and the Beast.* Illustrated by Mercer Mayer. Four Winds, 1978.
Full-color paintings intensify the mood of the familiar, haunting tale. (Objective 5)

Nakano, Dokuohtei. *Easy Origami.* Viking, 1985.
Instructions are given for over fifty figures which children can fold from paper to use, play with, or display. (Objective 4)

Ness, Evaline. *Tom Tit Tot.* Charles Scribner's Sons, 1965.
Woodcuts heighten the humor of the British version of the Rumpelstiltskin tale. (Objective 5)

O'Neill, Mary. *Hailstones and Halibut Bones: Adventures in Color.* Illustrated by John Wallner. Doubleday, 1989.
A new edition of an old favorite evokes children's response to color, inviting a follow-up photography activity. (Objective 1)

Raboff, Ernest. *Frederic Remington.* Lippincott, 1973.
The western art of Frederic Remington is introduced through text and reproductions of his paintings and sculptures. (Objective 3)

Robbins, Ken. *At the Ballpark.* Viking, 1988.
A photographic essay recreates the excitement of attending a professional baseball game. (Objective 1)

Sakata, Hideaki. *Origami.* Harper & Row, 1984.
Photos and brief text illustrate the folding of 39 basic origami figures. (Objective 4)

Sattler, Helen Roney. *Recipes for Art and Craft Materials.* Lothrop, Lee & Shepard, 1973, 1987.
Instructions for making modeling dough that need not be cooked are included in this volume of art materials recipes. (Objective 3)

Small, David. *Paper John.* Farrar, Straus & Giroux, 1987.
Paperfolding as an art form is highlighted in the story of John, who folded paper to make his house and satisfy his worldly needs. (Objective 4)

Steptoe, John. *The Story of Jumping Mouse.* Lothrop, Lee & Shepard, 1984.
Graphite pencil and India ink drawings help recreate the Native American tale of the mouse who, through his compassion and perseverance, becomes an eagle. (Objective 2)

Van Allsburg, Chris. *The Garden of Abdul Gasazi.* Houghton Mifflin, 1979.
Black-and-white drawings heighten the eerie mood as Alan goes to a magician's house to retrieve Fritz, the naughty dog. (Objective 2)

Yolen, Jane. *The Emperor and the Kite.* Illustrated by Ed Young. Philomel, 1967.
Full-color illustrations based on an intricate Oriental paper-cutting technique are used to enhance the story of the emperor's daughter who saved her father's life. (Objective 4)

————. *The Seeing Stick.* Illustrated by Remy Charlip and Demetra Maraslis. Thomas Y. Crowell, 1977.
Color is added to the illustrations to emphasize the old man's success in teaching the emperor's blind daughter to see with her hands. (Objective 2)

Zelinsky, Paul O. *Rumpelstiltskin.* E.P. Dutton, 1986.
Oil paintings delineate the medieval German setting and dramatize the well-known Grimm tale. (Objective 5)

GROUP INTRODUCTORY ACTIVITY:

Preparation: Locate *Paper John* by David Small and Hideaki Sakata's *Origami.* Obtain squares of origami paper or other thin art paper. Using the directions on page 37 of *Origami,* fold a paper table.

Focus: Introduce David Small's *Paper John* by showing the class the paper table that was prepared earlier. Tell the children that this book is about a man who made his house and any objects he needed by folding paper. Ask children to discuss the advantages and disadvantages of creating needed household items from paper. Instruct the students that, as the story is read, they should notice all the items John created from paper. Note also that many are included in the illustrations that are not mentioned in the text. Tell the children to watch the illustrations and listen carefully to the text in order to discover a disadvantage John encountered.

Objective: To satisfy the objective of realizing how paperfolding and cutting can be used as an art form, read *Paper John* to the class.

Guided Activity: After reading *Paper John,* have the children recall items that John folded from paper. In what ways were those items useful to John? Which item from the book would they enjoy owning? Were there any items that the children feel would be better or more useful if made from another material? Ask children to recall the advantages and disadvantages they discussed earlier. If they did not include the possibility of the house and its furniture blowing away, that idea may be suggested.

Extending Activity: Give each child a square of origami or thin art paper. Teach children to fold a table like that shared earlier by following oral directions. Request that each child use the directions in *Origami* by Hideaki Sakata to create a household item from folded paper. Place the objects on display.

FOLLOW-UP ACTIVITIES FOR TEACHER AND STUDENTS TO SHARE:

1. Ask the children to make a pencil drawing of a tree as it might appear in late autumn. After the children have completed their sketches, tell the class that Jim Arnosky is an authority on drawing nature. Share pages 34–39 of Jim Arnosky's *Sketching Outdoors in Autumn* in which he gives suggested techniques for drawing autumn trees. Emphasize the importance of observation in order to include small details that give a realistic sense to the drawing. Have the children each take a pencil and paper, go outside as a group, and while carefully observing a tree, make a pencil sketch. After returning to their room, they may want to add shading and detail. Have children compare their first and second sketches and write a short paragraph evaluating the effect of their careful observation upon the drawings they created. If the season in which this activity is used is not autumn, use appropriate pages from Jim Arnosky's *Sketching Outdoors in Spring* (Lothrop, Lee & Shepard, 1987), *Sketching Outdoors in Summer* (Lothrop, Lee & Shepard, 1988), or *Sketching Outdoors in Winter* (Lothrop, Lee & Shepard, 1987).

2. Introduce paper folding as an art technique by telling the story of Molly Bang's *The Paper Crane*, allowing the children to examine the illustrations as the story is told. Tell the children that the Japanese word for "paperfolding" is "origami." Through its frequent use "origami" has become an accepted English word as well. Using the directions in *Origami* by Hideaki Sakata, teach the children to fold a paper crane. Attach string to the completed cranes and hang them from the ceiling as mobiles.

3. Before sharing Byrd Baylor's *When Clay Sings*, ask the class if anyone can suggest why she titled the book as she did. After children respond to the question, tell the class that they are to listen to the figurative language of the text and study the illustrations by Tom Bahti so that they will be able to answer more confidently after the story is completed. Following the reading of the book, call attention to the map showing areas where the prehistoric Native American pottery was unearthed. Share the text on that page with the students. Now let children discuss the meaning of Baylor's title.

    As a follow-up, use a clay or dough recipe such as one found in Helen Sattler's *Recipes for Art and Craft Materials* to prepare a clay compound. Have the children design and create a shard suggestive of prehistoric Native American pottery. The children may want to use designs from Baylor's book or research in the media center for other appropriate designs and more information about the methods used by primitive or early potters.

If possible, arrange a field trip to a local potter's shop, or invite a potter to demonstrate his or her craft in the classroom. If children were successful in their research on early pottery methods, urge them to compare and contrast that information with their observations of modern techniques.

4. Introduce Paul Fleischman's *The Animal Hedge* by asking the children if they have ever heard of topiary gardening. Explain that topiary is a gardening technique in which plants are sculpted, trimmed, or trained into ornamental shapes. Ask students how they think a topiary gardener decides what shape each piece should take. Accept the children's ideas and, if needed, suggest that the natural growth of the plant, its purpose or placement, and use of prepared forms for the plant to grow on may influence the decision. Read *The Animal Hedge,* asking children to pay close attention to the illustrations by Lydia Dabcovich. After the book is completed, discuss what caused the hedge to appear as it did for the farmer and his sons.

   As a follow-up, ask the students to think about their own wishes for future occupations. Ask children to use a piece of green clay to sculpt a "topiary hedge" that in some way represents their chosen occupation. Display their sculptures.

5. Introduce Robert Froman's *Seeing Things* by sharing the first concrete poem, "A Seeing Poem." After reading, call attention to the fact that this poem uses letter size and placement rather than line drawings to create the shape. Now share "Homeweb," page 11, and "At the Dentist's," page 20. Let children talk about how the partial line drawings add to the effectiveness of the poems. Then share "Graveyard," page 24, and "Telephone Pole," page 46. Have children talk about the value of adding lines to some concrete poems to enlarge the meaning. Ask each child to write a concrete poem, using pencil lines as well as arrangement of words to indicate the subject.

6. Introduce *Snow-White and the Seven Dwarfs* illustrated by Nancy Ekholm Burkert, telling the students that she used her own 14-year-old daughter as the model for Snow-White. To add authenticity to the illustrations she did research in a medical library to discover the physical characteristics and proportions of dwarfs in order to present them as real people. Ask the class to note the illustrations of the

dwarfs' home because many of the items were copied from museum pieces. Suggest that the children study the details of the illustrations carefully as the story is told. After sharing the story, ask the children to recall details of the illustrations that particularly impressed them. If the children do not note that the face of the stepmother is not shown, draw attention to that fact. Ask them to speculate why Burkert chose not to illustrate the woman's face.

As a follow-up, ask the children who are interested to read *Snow White* illustrated by Trina Schart Hyman. Ask them to write responses to the following questions: a. What specific details in the illustrations add to the suspense of the story? b. How does the color choice in the Burkert and Hyman editions affect the mood of each book? c. Which illustrations do you prefer and why?

7. Introduce Tana Hoban's *Shadows and Reflections* by asking the class if they can think of instances in which photographs would be more appropriate than drawings or other forms of illustration. Children may suggest that photographs may be preferable to display emotion, to present accurate details, to identify people, and to document places one has visited. Tell the children that Tana Hoban's textless book *Shadows and Reflections* uses photographs of actual objects to present the concepts. As the class shares each picture, have them point out the shadows and reflections. In addition, have them notice how Hoban framed the picture to draw attention to specific details. Let them discuss how Hoban's artist's eye results in their seeing usual objects in an unusual way.

As a follow-up, have an amateur or professional photographer (media specialist, photo club member, camera shop employee, etc.) make a presentation to the class on how to take effective pictures. After the presentation, divide the class into groups of five or six and let them think of a concept or theme they could present with captioned or uncaptioned photographs. Have them plan and take twelve slide exposures to illustrate their idea, being sure all children take at least one photograph. Let the groups share their slide presentations, making an audio tape to accompany it if any captioning is needed.

8. Introduce Kathryn Lasky's *Dinosaur Dig* by asking the class why people take a camera along on vacations. Tell the children that this book records a trip from Cambridge, Maine, to Montana. The author's family made the trip in order to take part in a dinosaur dig. Kathryn Lasky's husband took the pictures that are included in the

book. In order to make the illustrations more meaningful, use a large map of the United States to trace the route the family took. While the illustrations are shared and the captions read, the class should follow the pictures carefully. As a follow-up, the class will plan and document with photographs a field trip they will take.

After sharing the book, schedule an appropriate field trip. Plan the pictures students feel they will need to take during the trip. On the actual trip each child should take at least one photograph. After the pictures are developed, the class may sequence the pictures, write appropriate captions, and place them in a class scrapbook.

9. To introduce the "cowboy art" of Frederic Remington, share the first two pages of his biography by Ernest Raboff. Inform the children that he is remembered for his sculpture as well as his paintings. Share the text and reproductions of "Bronco Buster," "Coming through the Rye," and "The Stampede." Discuss with the students the fact that sculptures are three-dimensional and in reality may be viewed from any angle. Ask the children to speculate whether it would be more difficult for them to create a sculpture or a painting. Urge them to justify their answers. After the children carefully examine the illustrations, ask them to discuss why Remington was called an artist-historian. Suggest that children read the book and complete the related individual activities on their own.

10. Introduce John Steptoe's *The Story of Jumping Mouse* by telling students that this book was chosen as a Caldecott Honor book in 1985. Ask them to recall the meaning and significance of the Caldecott Medal (as presented in the "Media and Methods" unit, Chapter 2). Explain to the children that this Native American tale is illustrated in black and white and uses light and shadow instead of color to add realism to the pictures. Ask the children to notice the graphite pencil and India ink illustrations. For added dramatic effect, practice reading the story with an appropriate musical background, such as the first movement of Dvorak's *Symphony in E Minor, Op. 95*, "From the New World," (Allegro, ACS 8008, 40 min., sound cassette). Share the illustrations as the book is read. After completing the reading, ask the children to recall their favorite picture. Turn to a few of the ones they suggest and ask the children to describe why the drawing was so memorable.

11. Before sharing Jane Yolen's *The Emperor and the Kite*, explain to the students that Ed Young's illustrations were created based on an Oriental paper-cutting technique. Ask the students to examine the

illustrations carefully as the story is read. After completing the book, ask the children if they believe these illustrations would be easy to create. Why or why not?

Suggest to the students that they make a dragon whose body is formed by using a simple paper-cutting technique. Give each child a strip of thin art paper approximately 3" x 11" in size. Ask the children to accordian fold the paper, making five to six folds across the 11" length to produce a rectangle that is approximately 3" x 2". Ask the children to cut two wedge-shaped pieces from one folded edge and two wedge-shaped pieces from the opposite folded side. Be sure to leave widths of the fold between the wedges. Unfold the paper, which is now the dragon's body. Attach the bodies to contrasting paper. Design and create a dragon's head to be attached to the body.

12. Ask if anyone can recall the story of Rumpelstiltskin. After a brief sharing session, tell the children that the familiar story which included spinning straw into gold appeared first in the Grimm Brothers' 1819 edition of *Children's and Household Tales.* Paul Zelinsky's version uses a medieval setting for the illustrations and retains the basic elements of the German tale. Suggest that each of Zelinsky's oil paintings is itself a work of art, full of detail. Tell them that, as the tale is read, they should note the illustrations and the use of color to evidence the change of mood in the story. After completing the book, allow children to discuss the mood as reflected in the pictures. Ask them to recall the colors used as the servant searches for the little man. What colors were evident at the end of the story? Have them discuss details in the illustrations that reinforce the story (e.g., spools of gold thread).

In the next session read the English version of the Rumpelstiltskin tale, *Tom Tit Tot,* illustrated in woodcuts by Evaline Ness. Ask the children what adjectives they would use to describe this version of the tale. If the children do not say the story was humorous, draw out this response from them. Ask the children to suggest which, if any, of the woodcut illustrations added to the story. Have the students compare the illustrations in the Zelinsky and Ness versions. Would each book have been as successful if the other style and medium of illustration had been used?

FOLLOW-UP ACTIVITIES FOR INDIVIDUAL STUDENTS:

1. After Jim Arnosky's *Sketching Outdoors in Autumn* has been shared as a class activity, read page 10 on drawing an animal's footprint and study the illustration on page 11. Search for an animal footprint near your home and use Arnosky's suggestions to sketch the print with a soft pencil. Share the sketch with the class. See if anyone can identify the animal by its footprint.

2. Read the introduction, pages 10–13, of Joan Irvine's *How to Make Pop-Ups*. Select a project you would like to create. Follow the directions. Share the completed project with the class and briefly explain how it was done.

3. After sharing Tana Hoban's *Shadows and Reflections* in class, read *A Very Young Gymnast* by Jill Krementz. Examine the pictures carefully as you read. Select ten photographs and write a caption for each that adds to rather than repeats the text.

4. After sharing Kathryn Lasky's *Dinosaur Dig* and taking a field trip, choose *Dinosaur Dig* from the reading table and read the book. Have adults at home help you arrange pictures of a trip you have taken. Write captions for each. Bring them to school and display them in a safe place suggested by the teacher. Place the captions below each picture so viewers can gain meaning from the photographs.

5. After the photographs by Tana Hoban in *Shadows and Reflections* are introduced in class, read Patricia Lauber's *Volcano: The Eruption and Healing of Mount St. Helens*. Study the illustrations and captions carefully as you read the text. Now go back and select five particularly informative illustrations. Identify each by page number. In a brief paragraph justify why each illustration was essential in order to gain full meaning from the text.

6. After the class has shared Molly Bang's *The Paper Crane*, examine Dokuohtei Nakano's *Easy Origami*. For background information on origami, read the introduction and directions on pages 4–6. Then select a page on which directions for an origami project are given. Fold the object and share it with the class, explaining the folding technique.

7. After sharing Paul Zelinsky's *Rumpelstiltskin* and *Tom Tit Tot* by Evaline Ness in class, go to the school media center and find Jan Brett's illustrated version of *Beauty and the Beast* and Marianna Mayer's *Beauty and the Beast*, illustrated by Mercer Mayer. Read both versions and study the illustrations carefully. Write a paragraph justifying which illustrations you prefer.

8. Following the class study of Tana Hoban's *Shadows and Reflections*, read Mary O'Neill's *Hailstones and Halibut Bones*. Using her ideas of writing poetry about colors, select a color and take photographs to illustrate it instead of using paintings as John Wallner did for O'Neill's book. Write an original color poem that includes those objects you photographed. Copy your poem on a large sheet of paper and arrange the photographs attractively around it for a class display.

9. After completing *Frederic Remington* by Ernest Raboff in class, re-examine the text and reproduction of "The Mystery of the Buffalo Gun." Write a paragraph discussing any historical facts you learned and why the painting has the words "The Mystery" in the title. Compare this painting with the sculpture "The Stampede." Write a second paragraph comparing and contrasting the two. Especially note the artist's depiction of the animals in both works.

10. After sharing Tana Hoban's *Shadows and Reflections* in class, read *At the Ballpark* by Ken Robbins. Study the pictures and the brief text before answering the following questions:
   a. Did the pictures sufficiently present the game or would you have preferred a longer text?
   b. Do the photographs adequately express the excitement of attending a professional baseball game? Justify both answers.

11. After sharing Molly Bang's *The Paper Crane* in class and folding a paper crane, examine Hideaki Sakata's *Origami*. Select one origami figure from the book, get a square of paper from the teacher, and follow the directions to fold the object. Share your finished product with the class and demonstrate how you folded the figure.

12. Make one of the recipes for preparing modeling dough and clay on pages 41–43 of Helen Sattler's *Recipes for Art and Craft Materials*. Use the product you created to sculpt an animal or object. Label and display your sculpture in the classroom.

13. As you read Chris Van Allsburg's *The Garden of Abdul Gasazi*, examine the border around the text and the black-and-white illustrations. Note the dog Fritz, Van Allsburg's pet, who appears in more than one of the author's books. After completing the book, use a soft pencil to draw a picture of your pet or one you would like to own. Use the pencil to shade the picture, creating areas of light and dark rather than a mere line drawing. Create an appropriate pencil border to frame your drawing.

14. Read Jane Yolen's *The Seeing Stick.* Study the illustrations by Remy Charlip and Demetra Maraslis. Most of the book is illustrated in black-and-white pencil drawings. Write a brief paragraph in which you speculate about why the artist chose to use color for a few of the illustrations.

PART II
Music Programs

Chapter 4
Music: Kindergarten/ Transition/First Grade

Timbre

OBJECTIVES:

1. Recognize families of instruments.
2. Discriminate between the major instruments in each family.
3. Realize that all the instrument families combine to form the orchestra.
4. Identify the conductor as the person who directs an orchestra or choir.

RECOMMENDED READINGS:

Haseley, Dennis. *The Old Banjo.* Illustrated by Stephen Gammell. Macmillan, 1983.
Black-and-white illustrations set the mood for the story of a boy and his father who follow the sounds of instruments abandoned on the farm. (Objectives 1 and 2)
Hayes, Phyllis. *Musical Instruments You Can Make.* Illustrated by Dennis Kendrick. Franklin Watts, 1981.
Brief introductions to types of instruments are followed by simple directions for making each sound source. (Objectives 1 and 3)

Hurd, Thacher. *Mama Don't Allow: Starring Miles and the Swamp Band.* Harper & Row, 1984.

Watercolor illustrations add spark to the story of Miles and the Swamp Band who share their favorite song, for which the score is included. (Objectives 1, 2, and 3)

Kraus, Robert. *Musical Max.* Illustrated by Jose Aruego and Ariane Dewey. Simon and Schuster, 1990.

The reader is introduced to a variety of instruments as Max practices and is ultimately joined by his friends to form an orchestra. (Objectives 1, 2, 3, and 4)

Maxner, Joyce. *Nicholas Cricket.* Illustrated by William Joyce. Harper & Row, 1989.

The crickets form an unusual band to help the forest creatures celebrate the night. (Objective 3)

van Kampen, Vlasta and Irene C. Eugen. *Orchestranimals.* Scholastic, 1989.

The penguin conductor has trouble organizing his animal orchestra in time for the concert. (Objectives 1, 2, 3, and 4)

GROUP INTRODUCTORY ACTIVITY:

Preparation: Locate *Musical Max* by Robert Kraus.   Obtain several instrument catalogs from local music stores or instrument companies.

Focus: Ask the children if they can name any musical instruments. List their responses on the chalkboard. Tell the children that instrument sounds are usually created in one of three ways: by blowing in or on the instrument, by striking it, or by plucking or using a bow on the strings.

Objective: To fulfill the objectives of recognizing families of instruments, discriminating between instruments, realizing that families of instruments combine to form the orchestra, and identifying the conductor as one who directs the orchestra, review the list of instruments the children suggested earlier. Ask the class to identify those instruments from the list that produce sounds by being blown, those that are struck, and those that have strings. Tell the children that many instruments are included in *Musical Max* by Robert Kraus. Tell the children that, as the book is read, they are to watch Jose Aruego's and Ariane Dewey's illustrations to find any instruments listed earlier and at least one that has not been mentioned.

Guided Activity: Read *Musical Max* aloud. After completing the book, ask the children to recall any instruments that they had named for their list that were included in the book. Ask children to add other instruments from the book to the list. After the list is completed and children have identified the method of producing sound for each instrument, tell the children that groups of instruments which make sounds in the same way are called a family.

Let the class re-examine the final double-spread illustration in which all the animals join in playing. Have the children identify the instruments included that belong in each family. Ask children if they can tell what Max is doing. After the children identify that he is leading the group, tell them that the leader or director of a large musical group is called the conductor and that this group is an orchestra.

Extending Activity: Divide the children into three groups and assign each group a family of instruments that produces sounds in the same way. Let the children use instrument catalogs to cut or tear out pictures of various instruments that belong in the assigned family and glue them onto a large sheet of paper to create a "Musical Family Collage." If the class is very advanced, the children may be placed in four groups instead of three. Divide the instruments that produce sounds by being blown into the two more specific families of "brass" and "wind," and introduce the names "string" and "percussion" for the other families.

FOLLOW-UP ACTIVITIES FOR TEACHER AND STUDENTS TO SHARE:

1. Before sharing Dennis Haseley's *The Old Banjo*, ask the children to listen carefully to the words so they can recall the phrases used to describe how a particular instrument sounds (e.g., the trumpet "makes a sound like geese flying in on a winter's night"). After reading the book, have the children speculate about whether the instruments played a sad or happy song. If *The Old Banjo* were continued, what do the children think would have happened to the instruments? Let the children recall phrases from the book describing the sounds of the instruments. Play recorded excerpts from Benjamin Britten's *Young Person's Guide to the Orchestra* (Columbia MS6368, 1s, 12in, 33 rpm) that include some of the instruments in the book. Let the group discuss whether or not the phrase from Haseley's text accurately describes the timbre of each instrument heard.

2. Introduce Phyllis Hayes's *Musical Instruments You Can Make* by reading page 4 which discusses vibration and sound. Give each child a rubber band and let the students make the humming sound described in the text. Follow this activity by reading the one-paragraph introductions on pages 6, 8, 11, 14, 18, 20, 24, and 29 which present a number of instruments. After reading each paragraph and showing the illustration, have the children decide in what family of instruments each belongs (winds that are blown, percussion instruments that are hit or struck, or strings that are plucked or bowed). Ahead of time collect simple items necessary to create harmonicas, chimes, tambourines, flutes, and guitars according to the directions in the book. After each child has created an instrument, read the last page of the book which tells them they can now combine their instruments to form an orchestra. Play a simple song on the piano and allow the children to add their handmade orchestra sounds by playing the steady beat.

3. Before reading Thacher Hurd's *Mama Don't Allow: Starring Miles and the Swamp Band,* tell the children they are to watch the illustrations and listen carefully so they can recall the instruments in the Swamp Band. Read the book. Have the children list the instruments they remember and classify them by musical families. If any instruments were not recalled, show the appropriate illustration to jog the children's memories. Teach the students the Swamp Band's favorite song, "Mama Don't Allow." Let the children sing the verses. Follow with Hurd's suggestion from the final page that the children make up their own verses for the song, beginning with "Mama don't allow no foot stompin'." Urge children to participate in actions that are appropriate for the lyrics as the song is sung.

4. Have the children name instruments that might be included in a band. Introduce Joyce Maxner's *Nicholas Cricket* by telling the children that in this story an unusual band is formed. Ask them to listen to the words carefully as the story is read so they can identify the instruments the cricket used. If children are not able to identify the instruments after the story is completed, go back and reread the three lines beginning with "and the washboard strummers." As a follow-up, form a class cricket band, using washboards (a guiro may be used for a washboard), musical spoons (claves or rhythm sticks may be substituted), and kazoos. Simple kazoos may be made by rubber banding a 4" square of tissue paper to one end of a toilet paper roll. Let the children march around the room playing a favorite song on their cricket instruments.

5. Ask the children to notice the names of the various instruments and any facts they learn about each as Vlasta van Kampen's *Orchestranimals* is read. Tell them that the conductor introduces the families of instruments by talking about his musicians as "players to bow. . . players to blow and players to hit to the beat." Read *Orchestranimals*. Ask the children to recall instruments from the book. Have the class determine whether each instrument named is one to blow, bow, or hit to the beat.

Pitch and Dynamics

OBJECTIVES:

1. Participate in speaking and singing in unison.
2. Sing a melody with simple accompaniment.
3. Echo simple tonal patterns.
4. Identify loud and soft dynamic levels when heard.

RECOMMENDED READINGS:

Grimm Brothers. *The Bremen Town Musicians*. Illustrated by Josef Palecek. Picture Book Studio, 1988.
   Illustrations highlight the instruments the animals play in this traditional story of the animals who scare the robbers and find a home. (Objectives 1, 3, and 4)
Hush, Little Baby. Illustrated by Margot Zemach. E.P. Dutton, 1976.
   This edition contains the score of the traditional lullaby in which a baby is promised a number of things if he will be quiet. (Objectives 1 and 2)
Ivimey, John W. *The Complete Story of the Three Blind Mice*. Ilustrated by Paul Galdone. Clarion, 1987.
   This complete illustrated version of the familiar song has a happy ending. (Objectives 1, 2, and 3)
Raffi. *Shake My Sillies Out*. Illustrated by David Allender. Crown, 1987.
   Humorous illustrations extend the text of a simple action song with the melody line and chord accompaniment appended. (Objectives 1, 2, 3, and 4)

Shannon, George. *Lizard's Song.* Illustrated by Jose Aruego and Ariane Dewey. Greenwillow, 1981.
Lizard's song appeals to Bear so much that he wants to make it his own. (Objectives 1, 2, and 3)
Songs from Mother Goose. Compiled by Nancy Larrick. Illustrated by Robin Spowart. Harper & Row, 1989.
A collection of 56 rhymes with melody lines, illustrations, and historical notes. (Objectives 1, 2, and 3)
Zelinsky, Paul O. *Wheels on the Bus.* E.P. Dutton, 1990.
Movable parts in the illustrations highlight each verse of the familiar action song whose melody is on the back cover. (Objectives 1 and 4)

GROUP INTRODUCTORY ACTIVITY:

Preparation: Locate *The Bremen Town Musicians* by the Brothers Grimm, illustrated by Josef Palecek. Before sharing the book, develop a simple tonal pattern or melody for the call of each animal ("Hee-haw," "Bow-wow," "Me-ow," and "Cock-a-doodle-doo").

Focus: Show the children Palecek's cover illustration for *The Bremen Town Musicians.* Ask the children to speculate about what the animals are doing. Then point out that the mouths of the animals are open. Let them make the sound the animals might be making.

Objective: To satisfy the objectives of participating in unison singing, echoing simple tonal patterns, and identifying loud and soft dynamic levels, share *The Bremen Town Musicians.*

Guided Activity: After reading *The Bremen Town Musicians* to the class, introduce the tonal patterns developed earlier for each of the animal calls. Have the class echo the sounds until the children are secure with the pattern. Divide the class into four groups, one for each animal. Tell the children to make the sound that scared the robbers. Ask the groups to combine and softly sing their animal calls together. Then have the children perform the same sound loudly. Allow the class to speculate about which dynamic level the animals used to scare the robbers.

Extending Activity: After the animals frightened the robbers, they lived long and happily in their house. Undoubtedly they played the instruments mentioned in the story and sang together often. Let the children choose instruments from the classroom which they can use to accompany the singing of a favorite song.

FOLLOW-UP ACTIVITIES FOR TEACHER AND STUDENTS TO SHARE:

1. Teach the melody of the lullaby "Hush, Little Baby" by rote. When children are secure with the melody, share *Hush, Little Baby* illustrated by Margot Zemach. Invite the children to sing along. Show the illustrations and sing the verses. As a follow-up, change "If that horse and cart fall down," to "If that horse and cart won't go." Let the children think of a new last line to complete the verse. Urge the children to think of at least one more verse for the song that would follow the new ending.

2. Before sharing with the students, practice singing John W. Ivimey's *The Complete Story of the Three Blind Mice,* fitting the text to the familiar melody on the back cover of the book. Share the song with the students, showing Paul Galdone's illustrations as the song is sung. Share the book again, this time asking the children to echo the repetitive lines.

3. Introduce Raffi's *Shake My Sillies Out* by telling the children that this book tells the story of three animals who can't sleep and meet a group of campers. Ask them to watch the illustrations carefully as the story is read. After completing the text, let the children briefly discuss the story they saw depicted in the illustrations. Reread the book, urging children to join in speaking the repeated lines of the text. Teach the melody of the song by having the children echo each line of the first verse. When the group has mastered the lyrics, sing the entire song in unison.

   As a follow-up activity, let half the class act out the song while the remaining group sings the lines softly. Then reverse the groups and share the song again, singing loudly. Ask the children to decide whether, if one were shaking the sillies out, it would be more appropriate to sing softly or loudly.

4. Before sharing *Lizard's Song* by George Shannon, learn the simple melody the author includes at the end of the book. Teach the melody to the children by having them echo the tonal pattern of each line. Tell the class that in the story Lizard tries to teach the song to Bear. Ask the children to join in as the song is shared within the story. Read *Lizard's Song.*

   As a follow-up ask the children to suggest a different animal that might wish to sing Lizard's song. Let the class sing the song as that animal might share it (e.g., for a bird, "nest is my home."). After a number of animals are shared, the children may want to insert the name of their home town to make the song their own. The singing may be accompanied on an autoharp or other instrument.

5.   Introduce the book *Songs from Mother Goose* by telling the children that the book contains familiar nursery rhymes. Ask the class to study the illustration on page 14 to see if anyone can guess the rhyme that is illustrated. Ask the children to repeat the lines of "Jack and Jill" in unison. The melody may be taught by singing one line at a time and having the group echo by repeating each line after it is sung.

As time allows or on subsequent days, share "Pease Porridge Hot," p. 28. After children have mastered the words and melody, have them play out the clapping game described in the notes on p. 68. Choose other favorite rhymes to share with the class throughout the unit and conclude the study with "Here We Go Round the Mulberry Bush," p. 29. Have children sing and go through the motions as they go around in a circle. They may want to make up new verses and motions.

6.   Teach the first verse of *Wheels on the Bus* to the children by rote. Invite the class to listen carefully to the first line of each succeeding verse so they can join in as the remaining lines of the verse are sung. The children will enjoy observing the moving parts of the illustrations as they sing. As a follow-up, ask children if the babies on the bus cried loudly or softly. Then have children speculate about whether the mother's response was loud or soft. Let children sing the song again, using appropriate dynamic levels and adding hand motions instead of using the action parts in the illustrations. If the school library does not have this book with moving parts available, use Raffi's *Wheels on the Bus* (Crown, 1988).

Tempo and Rhythm

OBJECTIVES:

1.   Identify fast and slow as expressions of tempo.
2.   Understand that tempo can impart emotion or feeling.
3.   Demonstrate basic pulse through movement.
4.   Distinguish between like and unlike rhythm patterns.

RECOMMENDED READINGS:

Emberley, Barbara. *Drummer Hoff.* Illustrated by Ed Emberley. Prentice-Hall, 1967.
The snappy rhythm of the rhyming couplets invites children to march to the beat in this award-winning book. (Objective 3)

Martin, Bill, Jr. and John Archambault. *Chicka Chicka Boom Boom.* Illustrated by Lois Ehlert. Simon and Schuster, 1989.
The rhyming chant emphasizes rhythm as it shares the story of the alphabet that tries to climb a tree. (Objective 4)

Rosen, Michael. *We're Going on a Bear Hunt.* Illustrated by Helen Oxenbury. Macmillan, 1989.
Rhythm and tempo are emphasized as children participate in the search for a bear and the hasty retreat. (Objectives 1, 2, and 3)

Shannon, George. *Dance Away.* Illustrated by Jose Aruego and Ariane Dewey. Greenwillow, 1982.
Rabbit's rhythmic dance accelerates in tempo as he attempts to save his friends from Fox. (Objectives 1 and 3)

Singing Bee! A Collection of Favorite Children's Songs. Compiled by Jane Hart. Illustrated by Anita Lobel. Lothrop, 1982.
A comprehensive subject index which includes such topics as clapping songs, finger plays, and rounds enhances the use of this illustrated collection of 125 well-known children's songs with manuscripts for piano and guitar accompaniment. (Objective 4)

Van Laan, Nancy. *Possum Come a-Knockin'* Illustrated by George Booth. Alfred A. Knopf, 1990.
Rhythmic text and humorous illustrations describe the opossum's disrupting visit. (Objectives 1, 2, and 3)

GROUP INTRODUCTORY ACTIVITY:

Preparation: Locate Michael Rosen's *We're Going on a Bear Hunt.*

Focus: Read *We're Going on a Bear Hunt* to the children, showing them the illustrations as the story is read. Read at a faster pace that portion of the story that depicts the return trip.

Objectives: In order to fulfill the objectives of identifying fast and slow as expressions of tempo and understanding that tempo can impart feeling or emotion, hold a discussion of the book after it is read. Introduce the term' tempo as meaning the speed of motion or activity as well as the speed of a piece of music. In which part of the book was a fast tempo used? Ask the children to speculate about why the teacher read the last portion of the book at a faster pace. Did the illustrations give any clue to the emotions the hunters felt on the return journey? Reinforce with the class that the tempo of the reader's voice helps them to know the hunters are afraid and are running from the bear.

Guided Activity: Have children participate in the bear hunt by using body percussion and motions. This will satisfy the objective of demonstrating basic pulse through movement. Have a child or another adult display the illustrations and turn the pages as the teacher signals to do so. Have the children echo line by line (repeating the words and motions in the same manner the teacher or leader introduces). All motions are to be done in a steady rhythm. For all pages with the text "We're going on a bear hunt," use alternating pats on the legs to represent walking feet. While repeating "Swishy swashy!", extend both hands to the front and push out to the sides in a breast-stroke manner. "Splash splosh!" may be accompanied by the action of a swimming crawl stroke. "Squelch squerch!" can be portrayed by sliding the two hands together as if scooting through mud. For "Stumble trip" the leader may wish to pat the legs for "stumble" and roll the hands in front of the body for "trip." "Hooo wooo!" may be represented by cupping the hands around the mouth on "hooo" and extending the arms up and outward on "wooo!" In the cave do "Tiptoe!" by touching the legs with fingertips rather than patting with the entire hand. Use no motions from "What's that?" to "It's a bear!!!!" On the return trip use the appropriate motions, still in rhythm, but at a faster tempo.

Extending Activity: As a follow-up, have children think of other things they might encounter on a bear hunt and motions that could be done to represent them. Repeat the bear hunt activity without the book, using the children's suggestions as well as some of those from Rosen's book.

FOLLOW-UP ACTIVITIES FOR TEACHER AND STUDENTS TO SHARE:

1. Read Barbara Emberley's *Drummer Hoff* to the class, asking the children to notice Ed Emberley's illustrations. After hearing the story, ask the children to tap the steady beat on their legs as the book is read again. This time emphasize the word "but" and have children join in unison with the line "Drummer Hoff fired it off." On a succeeding day repeat the story, having the children march as the

verse is read. This time after the last "but Drummer Hoff fired it off" is read, stop marching. Insert the words "Ready" and "Aim" before "Fire! Kahbahblooom," all of which are to be repeated in rhythm.

2. Before sharing *Chicka Chicka Boom Boom* by Bill Martin, Jr. and John Archambault with the class, practice reading the rhyming text. Teach the group the couplet, "Chicka chicka boom boom! Will there be enough room?" before reading the book to the children. Have the children pat the rhythm pattern of the lines on their knees as they chant. Point to the children as the story is read so they can say the lines in unison at the appropriate time. Ask the children to listen to hear if all the lines in the book use the same rhythm pattern as the memorized couplet. After completing the book, reread the first two pages. Let the group discuss the rhythm patterns they heard and determine if they are like or unlike the couplet. See if students can recall any lines that share a like pattern.

3. Before reading George Shannon's *Dance Away*, share the title of the book. Tell the children that, after it is read, they will be asked to suggest why the author gave the story that title. Encourage the children to join in on the words of the dance as soon as they are familiar with the lines. After reading the book, let children speculate on the reason behind the title. Why do the children suppose the song went faster and faster as the rabbits danced with the fox? Introduce the word "tempo" to the class by telling them that this musical term refers to the speed of the music or beat. As a follow-up activity, reread the story and let the children use creative movement to demonstrate the beat and tempo of Rabbit's dance. Lead the children in the interpretation of Rabbit's dance determined by the text.

4. Share the fingerplay "Where Is Thumbkin," on page 29 in *Singing Bee!* Invite the children to use their fingers to join in the motions as directed at the bottom of the page while the song is shared. Teach the song and motions to the children by rote. After the class has mastered the text, ask the students to tap the rhythm of the words with their fingertips as the first verse of the song is repeated. Ask the children if the rhythm pattern stayed the same or changed during the song. See if anyone can recall a phrase in the words that has a different pattern from "Where is Thumbkin (e.g., "Here I am")." Have the entire class clap or tap the rhythm patterns in both phrases and compare the two to determine if they are like or unlike patterns. Follow the same procedure to teach "Five Little Chickadees," page 77, identifying like and unlike rhythm patterns in the song.

5. Before introducing Nancy Van Laan's *Possum Come a-Knockin'* to the children, practice reading the text until it can be read rhythmically to a steady beat. Set a metronome to the desired tempo and ask children to keep the beat by knocking on a chair or table (in time with the metronome) as the book is read. After completing the book, reset the metronome to a slower tempo. Urge the children to keep time again as the book is read at the slower pace. Ask the class to identify whether this was a sad or funny story. Have the children choose which tempo, fast or slow, is more appropriate for the humorous tone of the story.

Form and Style

OBJECTIVES:

1. Recognize the terms introduction, verse, and chorus (refrain) as traditional names for sections of a song form.
2. Learn simple folk songs.
3. Identify songs as being appropriate for a specific holiday or season.

RECOMMENDED READINGS:

Child, Lydia Maria. *Over the River and through the Wood.* Illustrated by Brinton Turkle. Scholastic, 1974, 1987.
Period illustrations are appropriate for this 1844 poem which includes the musical score and many unfamiliar verses. (Objective 3)

Greene, Carol. *The Thirteen Days of Halloween.* Illustrated by Tom Dunnington. Children's Press, 1983.
In this parody of "The Twelve Days of Christmas" typical Halloween items such as ghosts, bats, and goblins are the gifts. (Objective 3)

Jingle Bells. Illustrated by Maryann Kovalski. Little, Brown, 1988.
A humorous story line and whimsical illustrations revolve around the singing of the first verse and chorus of the seasonal song for which the melody line is included. (Objectives 1 and 3)

Langstaff, John. *Over in the Meadow.* Illustrated by Feodor Rojankovsky. Harcourt, Brace & World, 1957.
The musical manuscript is included for this counting rhyme based on an old folk song. (Objective 2)

The Lap-Time Song and Play Book. Edited by Jane Yolen. Illustrated by
Margot Tomes. Harcourt Brace Jovanovich, 1989.
Simple movement directions are included for sixteen familiar play
rhymes, of which ten include music. (Objective 2)

Mohr, Joseph. *Silent Night.* Illustrated by Susan Jeffers. E.P. Dutton, 1984.
Illustrations in muted colors emphasize the gentle mood of the familiar
German Christmas carol, with appended melody line. (Objective 3)

Old MacDonald Had a Farm. Illustrated by Glen Rounds. Holiday House,
1989.
Large-print text and humorous illustrations of each of Old MacDonald's
often unusual animals precede the musical score. (Objective 2)

Raffi. *The Raffi Christmas Treasury.* Illustrated by Nadine Bernard
Westcott. Crown, 1988.
Colorful, humorous illustrations and musical scores accompany this
collection of fourteen primarily secular Christmas songs. (Objective 3)

Staines, Bill. *All God's Critters Got a Place in the Choir.* Illustrated by
Margot Zemach. E.P.Dutton, 1989.
Watercolor illustrations add to the humor of this song with melody line
appended. (Objective 1)

This Old Man. Illustrated by Carol Jones. Houghton Mifflin, 1990.
Detailed illustrations with page cut-outs to help anticipate the action in
each verse are used to introduce this traditional English counting rhyme
with musical score included. (Objectives 1 and 2)

GROUP INTRODUCTORY ACTIVITY:

Preparation: Locate *This Old Man,* illustrated by Carol Jones.

Focus: Show the title page of *This Old Man,* illustrated by Carol Jones. Tell
the students that a circle is cut out on some of the pages to give a clue to the
action on the following page. Encourage children to share their ideas about
the clues as you read the story.

Objective: To fulfill the objectives of recognizing the terms introduction,
verse, and chorus as traditional names for sections of a song form and of
learning simple folk songs, share *This Old Man.*

Guided Activity: Read the book, inviting the group to join in on the
repeated lines as soon as they feel comfortable with the text. After
completing the story, introduce the terms introduction, verse, and chorus by
comparing these musical words to portions of the book. Explain that a
musical introduction is the portion of the music that comes first and means
"get ready, here comes the song." See if the children can pick out the title
page as the book's introduction to the text.

Remind children that one part of the words in *This Old Man* was repeated over and over. That portion could be called the chorus because the chorus is the part of a song that is repeated again and again. The lines that were different for each number from one to ten could be called the verse (because in a song the verse is that portion whose words change each time). Share the book again, singing the melody and inviting the class to join in singing the chorus.

Extending Activity: On subsequent days choose a student to share the illustrations of the book while the class sings along to a simple accompaniment. Remind the group of the musical terms "introduction," "verse," and "chorus" and their meanings. As the title page is shared, play a simple introduction to reinforce that concept. Urge children to join in singing as much of the song as possible while the appointed child shows the illustrations. Add motions to the chorus as follows: clap hands on "nick nack," pat alternate legs on "paddy whack," pantomime "give a dog a bone," and roll hands for "This old man came rolling home."

FOLLOW-UP ACTIVITIES FOR TEACHER AND STUDENTS TO SHARE:

1. Tell children they are going to hear a Thanksgiving song. Ask them to think about the words of the song so they can discuss whether they think the song was written recently or long ago. Sing the first verse of "Over the River and through the Wood" to the children. Allow the class to discuss word clues that made them know the song was written long ago. After their discussion tell the children that the words of the song were written in 1844 as "The Boy's Thanksgiving Day." Explain that the poem was later set to music and became a song.

    Introduce the book *Over the River and through the Wood* by Lydia Maria Child, telling the children to watch the pictures as you read the words of the song. Stop the reading to talk about the meaning of words they may not know, e.g., "dapple-gray." Discuss with the children how the Thanksgiving in the song was alike and different from their celebrations today. Teach the first verse of the song.

2. Introduce Carol Greene's *The Thirteen Days of Halloween* by playing the tune in the back of the book on a piano or other instrument. Ask children what holiday they think of when they hear that tune. Most children will identify the melody as a traditional Christmas song. Tell the children that Carol Greene has written a Halloween version of the "partridge in a pear tree." Ask the children to suggest Halloween symbols or animals that might be given as gifts. Read or sing *The Thirteen Days of Halloween.*

After completing the book, assign children the lines for each of the gifts and let the children practice their line until they are comfortable with it. Sing the song, letting the assigned children join in at the appropriate time. As a follow-up, let the children draw a picture of what they think was in the box that was the gift for the thirteenth day.

3. Ask the children if any of them know the chorus of "Jingle Bells." Sing the chorus and teach it by rote if necessary. Tell the class they are going to hear a humorous book about the song. Ask the children to sing the chorus when that part of the story is reached. Share the book, singing both the chorus and the verse when they appear. After completing the book, tell the class that the portion of the song beginning with "Dashing through the snow" is the first verse of the song. Although they were not included in the story, there are other verses. Teach the children the first verse of "Jingle Bells." If sleigh bells or jingle bells are available, have children play a steady beat on the bells as an eight-beat (two measures) introduction to the song. Allow the children to play the bells again as a rhythmic accompaniment to the chorus. To reinforce the concepts of verse and chorus, ask the children to hold the bells silently during the singing of the verse.

4. Introduce John Langstaff's *Over in the Meadow* by singing the song as the illustrations are shared. Teach the children the song. Let one group play out the story while the other group sings the song, using the illustrations as clues to the lyrics. Perform the song again, reversing the group roles.

5. Introduce Jane Yolen's *The Lap-Time Song and Play Book* by asking the children if anyone knows the words and actions to "I'm a Little Teapot," pages 12–13. If one or more children volunteer, allow them to demonstrate the song and motions to the class. Refine the motions and teach both song and actions to the rest of the group.

Jane Yolen suggests an alternate version of the song created by science-fiction writer Ed Bryant. Share those lines with the children and let them sing and act this version. When the children have mastered the melody, let the class make up a new rhyme for their own version of the folk song. On subsequent days other songs and play rhymes from the collection may be introduced.

6. Before sharing *Silent Night*, illustrated by Susan Jeffers, play a few bars of the song on the piano or other instrument. Ask the children if any of them recognize the music. Explain to the group that "Silent

Night" is one of the most widely known Christmas carols in the world. Then tell them that they are going to see a beautifully illustrated version of the song. As the children watch the illustrations in *Silent Night,* read or sing the lines. Teach the children the first verse of the song by rote.

7. Show the picture on the jacket or title page of *Old MacDonald Had a Farm,* illustrated by Glen Rounds. Tell the children that this man is a farmer. Ask if anyone knows the title of the song that this book is about. Sing the entire song, encouraging the children to join in singing the repeated lines. Share the pictures as each verse is sung. As a follow-up activity, have children think of other animals that might be on the farm. What sound is made by each animal? Using the suggested animals, let the class sing the new verses. Children may want to illustrate a new version of "Old MacDonald" with their created verses. These can be compiled into a class songbook with the teacher adding the lyrics to each page.

8. Introduce *The Raffi Christmas Treasury* by sharing the illustration on pages 46–47 as "We Wish You a Merry Christmas" is sung. Teach the song by rote to the children. Point out to the class that the singers in the book are watching the woman in the hot pink coat and yellow galoshes. Ask if anyone knows what that person is called. If children have already completed the "Timbre" unit, someone should recall that the leader of an orchestra or choir is called a conductor. If no one responds correctly, introduce the term again. Tell the children that a choir or orchestra must watch the conductor carefully as they perform. Act as the conductor and have the class stand and sing the song together. After learning and performing the song, children may want to listen to the audio cassette *Raffi's Christmas Album* (Kimbo 8116C, 1983, 31 min.) which contains "We Wish You a Merry Christmas" and the other songs in the book. After hearing the recording, children may want to select another song from the collection to learn.

9. Read *All God's Critters Got a Place in the Choir* by Bill Staines, allowing the children to enjoy the humorous illustrations. While sharing the illustrations a second time, sing the text to the melody included at the end of the book. Teach the chorus by rote. Sing the song again, letting the children join in on the chorus. Urge children to "clap their hands / Or paws / Or anything they got," as they sing.

Chapter 5
Music: Second Grade/
Third Grade

Timbre and Dynamics

OBJECTIVES:

1. Distinguish between various instruments and voices.
2. Participate in using body percussion to accompany songs or stories.
3. Create individual musical instruments.
4. Follow a director or conductor in expressing dynamic levels.

RECOMMENDED READINGS:

Ackerman, Karen. *Song and Dance Man.* Illustrated by Stephen Gammell.
   Alfred A. Knopf, 1988.
   Grandpa entertains his grandchildren with his song and dance routine
   from the days of vaudeville. (Objective 2)
Faulhaber, Martha and Janet Underhill. *Music: Invent Your Own.* Albert
   Whitman, 1974.
   Among the terms introduced are timbre and dynamics, with creative
   activities suggested for each. (Objectives 1 and 4)
Kuskin, Karla. *The Philharmonic Gets Dressed.* Illustrated by Marc
   Simont. Harper & Row, 1982.
   The reader can follow the members of the philharmonic orchestra as they
   prepare for a performance. (Objective 1)

Lillegard, Dee. *Brass.* Children's Press, 1988.
This introduction is enhanced by the color photographs of individuals playing each instrument as it is briefly described. (Objective 1)
———. *Percussion.* Children's Press, 1987.
Percussion instruments are illustrated with photographs and described briefly. (Objectives 1 and 3)
———. *Strings.* Children's Press, 1988.
Color photographs show children and adults playing the various string instruments described in the text. (Objective 1)
———. *Woodwinds.* Children's Press, 1987.
Brief descriptions of woodwind instruments are made more meaningful by color photographs. (Objectives 1 and 3)
Prokofiev, Sergei. *Peter and the Wolf.* Illustrated by Jorg Muller. Alfred A. Knopf, 1986. With accompanying cassette, ISBN 0-394-88418-3.
This picture book version of *Peter and the Wolf* is introduced by illustrations of each of the instruments that represent a character in the story and is available with an accompanying cassette performed by the Hamburg Symphony Orchestra. (Objectives 1 and 4)
Silverstein, Shel. *Where the Sidewalk Ends.* Harper & Row, 1974.
This poetry collection includes "Ourchestra," a humorous poem that inspires musical activity. (Objectives 2 and 3)
Wiseman, Ann. *Making Musical Things.* Charles Scribner's Sons, 1979.
Black-and-white drawings help clarify the directions for making more than fifty musical instruments, mostly from materials obtainable at home. (Objective 3)

GROUP INTRODUCTORY ACTIVITY:

Preparation: Locate Sergei Prokofiev's *Peter and the Wolf,* illustrated by Jorg Muller, and the accompanying cassette.

Focus: Tell the students they are going to hear a book version of Sergei Prokofiev's *Peter and the Wolf,* illustrated by Jorg Muller. After the story is read, they will listen to the story told by Prokofiev's music. Show the children the characters in the story and the instrument that will represent each.

Objective: In order to satisfy the objectives of distinguishing between various instruments and following a director or conductor in expressing dynamic levels, the student will become familiar with the plot of *Peter and the Wolf* and then listen to the orchestral piece.

Guided Activity: Share with the class the story of Sergei Prokofiev's *Peter and the Wolf*, illustrated by Jorg Muller. After completing the book, ask the children to listen carefully as the various musical instruments retell the story in the recorded version. Let the children listen to the audio cassette of *Peter and the Wolf* as the illustrations in the book are shown again. After completing the listening activity, again show the students the parade scene in the last double-spread illustration in the book. Point out the pictures of the conductor. Ask children to deduce from his gestures what dynamic level he is instructing the orchestra to use. If they are unable to respond, tell the group that large, broad movements are used to indicate a loud dynamic level while smaller gestures that are close to the body call for soft sounds.

Extending Activity: Let the children play out the story as they listen to Prokofiev's music.

FOLLOW-UP ACTIVITIES FOR TEACHER AND STUDENTS TO SHARE:

1. Read Karen Ackerman's story *Song and Dance Man*. Then reread the line, "His feet moved slowly at first, while his tap shoes made soft, slippery sounds like rain on a tin roof." Ask the children to demonstrate how they could use their hands on their legs to make a sound similar to the one described in the story. Suggest that the whole class pat their hands on their knees and then slide their hands up their legs in unison to make the tap and shuffle sound of the song and dance man's shoes. Turn the page and read the description of the step "that sounds like a woodpecker tapping on a tree." Let the children try to create that sound on their legs. The teacher may want to play a familiar song and let the children use the body percussion sounds used in *Song and Dance Man* to accompany the music. If any member of the class is taking tap lessons, perhaps he or she would like to bring tap shoes and demonstrate for the class.

2. Introduce *Music: Invent Your Own* by Martha Faulhaber and Janet Underhill by reading to the class page 15, which defines and illustrates the term "timbre." Continue with "The Timbre of Voice" on page 16. Let the children experience the timbre of voices by having one student stand with his or her back to the class. Point to another child who says or sings, "Whose voice is this?" or a similar question. The child standing must identify the speaker by the timbre of the voice. The speaker then stands and becomes the new listener. Give several students the opportunity to share.

Let children "Experiment with the Timbre of Different Objects," page 16, using previously collected materials. Tap each of the objects with a pencil or drumstick and listen to its unique timbre. Have a child turn his or her back to the class while another student taps an object. See if the child can identify the object by its timbre. As a follow-up, have the children do "Fun with Mother Goose," pages 17–19, or one of the other activities in this section.

On another day introduce the section on dynamics by reading the definition on page 37. Let students do the "Yankee Doodle" activity described on pages 38–39. Continue by letting one child be the conductor who will use the gestures demonstrated in the introductory activity to direct the group to use appropriate dynamics as they perform.

3. Start reading Karla Kuskin's *The Philharmonic Gets Dressed* without sharing the title of the book with the children. Read until the text and illustrations include the instrument cases. Stop reading and ask the children what they think the people in the book do. See if anyone can deduce why all the people were getting dressed in formal clothes. Continue reading until the text and illustration depict the conductor. Then let the children speculate why one person's case is different and why that person rides in a limousine.

Complete the book. Talk about the meaning of the word "philharmonic." Go back and examine the illustrations of the instruments. Have children identify each. Then let the class listen to Benjamin Britten's *Young Person's Guide to the Orchestra* (Columbia MS6368, 1s, 12in, 33 rpm). Keep the book open to the illustrations of the instruments. Let children point to each as the music is featured.

As a follow-up activity, ask children to design an original musical instrument and its carrying case. Name the instrument and write a two-sentence description of it, being sure to include the family to which it belongs. Post the designs, by families, on butcher paper or a large bulletin board labeled "Our Original Orchestra."

4. Tell the children that as Dee Lillegard's *Brass* is read, they should study the photographs carefully and listen to the descriptions of the instruments. After the book is read, go back to each photograph and ask the children to recall any fact that they remember about that instrument. Ask a local band instructor if someone who plays a brass instrument can visit the class, share his or her instrument, and play a selection for the class.

5. Ask the children to name some string instruments they know. Write on the board any instruments they list. Read Dee Lillegard's *Strings* to the class. After sharing the book, have the children recall additional string instruments to add to their list. Let the children discuss any facts they remember about each instrument.

    As a follow-up, introduce the class to the autoharp. Ask the students if the instrument reminds them of any string instrument from Lillegard's book. Tell the class that this instrument gets its name from the words "automatic" and "harp." It has many strings similar to a harp and the cross bars identified with chord symbols make it so simple that it almost seems to "play itself automatically." Teach the children to play a favorite folk song on the autoharp by strumming the strings to a steady beat while depressing the proper chord bars. In the days that follow, let the children take turns playing the autoharp while the rest of the class sings.

6. Read Dee Lillegard's *Percussion* to the children. Place the book in an activity area in the classroom. In the following days have each child select a favorite instrument from the book and draw a picture of it, label the instrument, and write a one-sentence description of it. As a follow-up, let children make castanets or tambourines. Use the directions on pages 16–17 of Ann Wiseman's *Making Musical Things* to make individual tambourines or use a suggestion from pages 42–43 of Wiseman's book to make castanets. Let children use these instruments to provide a percussion accompaniment to a favorite song.

7. Read *Woodwinds* by Dee Lillegard to the class. After completing the book, show the students the double-spread illustration of the four instrument families. Point out the five instruments included in a woodwind quintet (flute, oboe, clarinet, bassoon, and French horn). Explain to the children that the French horn, a brass instrument, is often included in the woodwind quintet because it has a more mellow sound than other brasses and it blends well with the woodwinds. As a follow-up, summarize "A Reeding Lesson," page 101 in Tom Walther's *Make Mine Music* (Little, Brown, 1981). Assist children in making simple drinking straw wind instruments as Walther suggests.

8. Share the poem "Ourchestra" from page 23 of Shel Silverstein's *Where the Sidewalk Ends*. Allow the children to discuss the meaning of the poem. Assign the children to play various body parts suggested in the poem and act out the poem as it is reread. As a follow-up, have the children make their own "fist kazoos" by

pressing their thumbs and closed forefingers against their mouths. Let them sing a song familiar to the class, substituting the neutral syllable "oo" for the words. (The activity will not work if the children use a closed-mouth hum.) Share two poems from Silverstein's book that have been made into songs. The musical version of "Boa Constrictor," page 45, may be found in *Peter, Paul, and Mommy* (Warner WS1785, 2s, 12in, 33rpm). The poem "The Unicorn," pages 76–77, has also been set to music and is included on the album *The Magical World of Roger Whittaker* (RCA AYL1-3670, 2s, 12in, 33rpm). This recording also contains a brief version of "Boa Constrictor."

9. Before sharing Ann Wiseman's *Making Musical Things*, have the children bring a coffee can with a plastic lid or an empty gallon plastic milk jug to school. Collect several extras for those children who are unable to bring their own. Read the poem on pages 6–7 of Wiseman's book. Suggest to the children that they use the items they brought from home as drums (page 18). Pencils with erasers can be used for drumsticks. Using Ann Wiseman's poem suggestion "Tap your street," have children tap the rhythm pattern of their street name on their drums. Let the children take turns performing their street addresses individually if they wish. Assist the children as needed. As a follow-up, create a simple rhythm pattern to a familiar song such as "Row, Row, Row Your Boat" and teach the children to play the repeated rhythm pattern over and over as an accompaniment. Divide the group in half and allow one group to play while the other sings.

Form and Style

OBJECTIVES:

1. Experience partner songs, repetitive songs, rounds, and cumulative songs.
2. Realize that program music tells a story through sound alone.
3. Identify terms which indicate the number of performers in a musical presentation.

RECOMMENDED READINGS:

Cole, Joanna. *Bony-Legs* Illustrated by Dirk Zimmer. Four Winds, 1983.
This action-filled retelling of a "Baba Yaga" story is enriched by detailed drawings. (Objective 2)

Kherdian, David and Nonny Hogrogian. *The Cat's Midsummer Jamboree.* Philomel, 1990.
As a mandolin-playing cat encounters other musical animals, they form a duet, trio, quartet, quintet, sextet, and, finally, a jamboree. (Objective 3)

Muller, Robin. *The Sorcerer's Apprentice.* Silver Burdett, 1985.
Muted illustrations impart a mysterious quality to the old folk tale. (Objective 2)

Nelson, Esther L. *The Silly Songbook.* Illustrated by Joyce Behr. Sterling, 1981.
Musical scores are included in this collection of humorous songs. (Objective 1)

Prelutsky, Jack. *Nightmares: Poems to Trouble Your Sleep.* Illustrated by Arnold Lobel. Greenwillow, 1976.
The texts of twelve ghoulish poems, including "The Dance of the Thirteen Skeletons," are made more startling by eerie black-and-white illustrations. (Objective 2)

Rounds, Glen. *I Know an Old Lady.* Holiday House, 1990.
Humorous illustrations will delight those who share this cumulative folk song. (Objective 1)

Westcott, Nadine Bernard. *Skip to My Lou.* Little, Brown, 1989.
Several verses of the traditional folk song are humorously illustrated to tell the tale of a young boy who is left in charge of the farm for a day. (Objective 1)

―――. *There's a Hole in the Bucket.* Harper & Row, 1990.
Illustrations add to the humor of the repetitive folk song about the man who gives excuses for not repairing a bucket. (Objective 1)

GROUP INTRODUCTORY ACTIVITY:

Preparation: Locate Joanna Cole's *Bony-Legs* and a recording of Modeste Mussorgsky's *Pictures at an Exhibition* (RCA LSC 3313, 2s, 12in., 33rpm).

Focus: Introduce the character of Baba Yaga by telling the children that she was a wicked witch in Russian folk tales. Show the class the book *Bony-Legs* and tell the students that Joanna Cole, the author, based the story on the Baba Yaga tales.

Objective: To satisfy the objective of realizing that program music tells a story through sound alone, the children will hear the story *Bony-Legs* and the excerpt "The Hut of Baba Yaga" from Mussorgsky's *Pictures at an Exhibition.*

Guided Activity: Read the book to the children. After completing the book, ask the children if they noticed anything unusual about Bony-Legs's house. After someone has pointed out that the house stands on chicken legs, tell the children that the house is shown in this way in all of the Baba Yaga stories. Explain that in some Baba Yaga stories the house can move on those legs when the old witch commands. Tell the children that a Russian composer, Modeste Mussorgsky, wrote a piece of music called "The Hut of Baba Yaga" (in *Pictures at an Exhibition*). This piece is called program music because it tells a story through music only, without words. Point out that in the music they can hear the hut limber up its legs, walk, and then run through the forest. Tell the children to listen for a change in the music when the hut begins to tiptoe. They will then hear Baba Yaga lean slowly from her window to grab a victim. Explain that the music ends with the hut running back to its clearing deep in the forest. Play the excerpt for the children.

Extending Activity: As a follow-up, play the excerpt again, letting students act out the motions of Baba Yaga and her hut as the children hear them in Mussorgsky's music.

FOLLOW-UP ACTIVITIES FOR TEACHER AND STUDENTS TO SHARE:

1. Read *The Cat's Midsummer Jamboree* by David Kherdian and Nonny Hogrogian, asking the children to notice the instruments and the musical terms indicating the number of performers in each group. After completing the book, show the illustrations of the groups of two, three, four, five, and six. Ask the children to identify the instruments played and recall the term that indicates the number in the group. Assist them as needed. As a follow-up, distribute various classroom instruments to the children and have a "mid-afternoon" or "mid-morning solo," "duet," "trio," "quartet," "quintet," "sextet," and a "jamboree" to a favorite song.
2. Read Robin Muller's *The Sorcerer's Apprentice* to the class. After completing the book, allow children to discuss the main elements of the story. Explain that many years ago Paul Dukas, a composer, wrote a piece of program music called *The Sorcerer's Apprentice.*

His music was based on an old ballad form of the folk tale that had been written by the poet Goethe. Explain to the children that folk tales often appear in several versions and that the story told by Goethe and Dukas is quite different from Muller's version. In order to acquaint the class with the story Dukas used, share with the children pages 4–6 of Lisl Weil's *The Magic of Music* (Holiday House, 1989). Have the children compare Weil's synopsis of the musical plot with that of the Muller retelling they heard earlier.

Before playing Dukas's music for the class, explain that Weil omitted a part of the story that they can plainly hear in the music. Tell the children that, when the apprentice discovers he cannot stop the enchanted broom, he finally chops it to pieces with an ax. Point out that this only works for a short time because each of the enchanted pieces comes to life and all begin to carry water. Play a recording of *The Sorcerer's Apprentice* (Columbia, BOL #59, 1s, 12in., 33rpm) for the students, asking them to listen carefully for the sound of the ax blows and other musical themes that represent major parts of the story.

3. Introduce "There's a Hole in the Bottom of the Sea" from Esther Nelson's *The Silly Songbook*, pages 90–91, by telling the children that this is a cumulative folk song. Explain that a cumulative folk song is one which accumulates or adds on additional words with each verse. Then it repeats the lines from all the previous verses. Teach the first verse by rote. The children can easily join in succeeding verses after hearing the first line of each.

As a follow-up, assign small groups of children to prepare the illustrations for each of the verses, adding the appropriate lines as a caption for the picture. Compile the illustrations in order to create an illustrated songbook, *There's a Hole in the Bottom of the Sea*. On a later day introduce another cumulative song, "Today Is Monday," pages 72–73, in a similar manner. The school cafeteria menu for the coming week may be substituted for the foods listed in the songbook.

On another day introduce the concept of rounds by sharing the round "Lasagna," page 83. Explain the term "round" as a song in which two or more groups sing a melody but begin at different points so that each group is a line behind the previous one. Teach "Lasagna" by rote and divide into two groups to sing the song. If the children enjoy this song they may want to learn the round "Grasshoppers Three," page 94.

4. Read to the children "The Dance of the Thirteen Skeletons" from Jack Prelutsky's *Nightmares: Poems to Trouble Your Sleep*, pages 34–38. Ask the students to retell the plot of the poem. Tell the children that this same basic story has been told in a piece of program music by Camille Saint-Saëns called "Danse Macabre." Repeat the lines from the poem:

> "And they dance in their bones,
>
> in their bare bare bones,
>
> with the click and the clack
>
> and the chitter and the chack
>
> and the clatter and the chatter
>
> of their bare bare bones."

Ask the children what musical instrument Saint-Saëns could have chosen to represent the click and the clack of the "bare, bare bones." After discussing appropriate instruments, tell the class that Saint-Saëns chose the xylophone to portray the rattling skeletons. Have them listen to the first portion of "Danse Macabre" (Columbia, BOL #59, 1s, 12in., 33rpm). Ask the children to raise their hands when they hear the skeletal bones dancing. Play the recording again, letting children improvise a skeleton dance as they listen.

5. Introduce cumulative folk songs by reading Glen Rounds's version of *I Know an Old Lady*. Share the musical version found on pages 131–133 of *Go In and Out the Window* (Henry Holt, 1987) and teach the children to sing the song. See if the children can recall any differences in this version and the book by Glen Rounds. Children may notice that Rounds includes a goat but no cow, and many of the lyrics are different.

Point out that the difference in the words occurs because, like folk tales, folk songs have been handed down from generation to generation and therefore exist in many forms. Tell the children that this is a cumulative folk song because in each verse it adds a new line while repeating the lines from the previous verses. Children may want to make flannelboard figures or puppets of the old lady and the animals and sing the song for a first-grade or kindergarten class while enacting the story with the figures.

6. Introduce Nadine Westcott's *Skip to My Lou* by asking how many of the children know the old folk song about "Flies in the sugarbowl, Shoo fly shoo." If any children recognize the words, see if they can

recall the name of the song or the rest of the verse. Show the children Nadine Westcott's book and tell them that this is an illustrated version of the song "Skip to My Lou." Ask the children to watch the pictures carefully to see how Nadine Westcott wove the verses together to create a story. Tell the children that the song will be sung rather than read. They may join in the singing when they recognize the pattern of repetition in the words and melody.

After completing the song, let the children discuss the plot of the story Nadine Westcott illustrated. What problems did the little boy face and how were they solved? As a follow-up, have the class think of another animal that could have been on the farm. Have them make up a new verse to indicate how that animal could have created a problem.

7.   Share Nadine Westcott's illustrations in *There's a Hole in the Bucket* as the song is sung for the children. Use the melody from the manuscript at the end of the book. Teach the children the first verse by rote. Introduce the term "partner songs" as referring to songs that are designed to be sung by two or more alternating voices. Have the girls sing Liza's line and the boys sing Henry's response. The children can easily learn the additional verses on succeeding days so they can share the entire book in partner song style. Share the song with another class or sing it in a program for parents.

Folk Songs Around the World

OBJECTIVES:

1.   Experience examples of music and dance that were included in the American heritage.
2.   Learn folk songs of various countries.
3.   Determine how folk songs grew out of the history of a people.

RECOMMENDED READINGS:

Arroz con Leche: Popular Songs and Rhymes from Latin America. Illustrated by Lulu Delacre. Scholastic, 1989.
Authentic illustrations extend the Spanish and English versions of a variety of Latin American songs and rhymes, several of which include musical scores. (Objectives 2 and 3)

The Fox Went Out on a Chilly Night. Illustrated by Peter Spier. Doubleday, 1961, 1989.
Illustrations of the New England countryside enhance this old folk song with the musical score appended. (Objectives 1 and 2)

Go Tell Aunt Rhody. Illustrated by Aliki. Macmillan, 1974, 1986.
Gouache illustrations vividly portray the lyrics of the song and allow the reader to extend the action beyond the text. (Objectives 1, 2, and 3)

Langstaff, John. *Frog Went a-Courtin'.* Illustrated by Feodor Rojankovsky. Harcourt Brace Jovanovich, 1955.
Caldecott Award-winning illustrations add to the humor of the familiar ballad with appended musical score. (Objectives 2 and 3)

London Bridge Is Falling Down! Illustrated by Peter Spier. Doubleday, 1967.
The history of London Bridge is included in this illustrated song containing eighteen verses. (Objective 3)

Martin, Bill, Jr. and John Archambault. *Barn Dance!* Illustrated by Ted Rand. Henry Holt, 1986.
A little boy discovers the animals barn dancing on a summer night. (Objective 1)

Sally Go Round the Moon. Compiled by Nancy and John Langstaff. Illustrated by Jan Pienkowski. Revels, 1970, 1986.
The origins of these American and international folk songs are indicated above the score, and simple movements are suggested for many of them. (Objectives 1 and 2)

The Twelve Days of Christmas. Illustrated by Jan Brett. G.P. Putnam's Sons, 1986, 1989.
Fanciful, detailed illustrations portray the lyrics of the cumulative English Christmas song, which is introduced by the musical score. (Objective 2)

GROUP INTRODUCTORY ACTIVITY:

Preparation: Locate *Go Tell Aunt Rhody,* illustrated by Aliki.

Focus: Introduce Aliki's illustrated version of *Go Tell Aunt Rhody* by sharing the history of the song given on the last page of the book.

Objective: To accomplish the objectives of experiencing examples of music and dance that were included in the American heritage, learning folk songs of various countries, and determining how folk songs grew out of the history of a people, share Aliki's illustrated songbook *Go Tell Aunt Rhody.*

Guided Activity: Sing the verses of *Go Tell Aunt Rhody* (including the repetitions) while showing Aliki's illustrations to the children. Share the textless illustrations that follow the last verse and have the children tell the story of what happened after the goose died. Explain to the children that this song reflects a time in American history when people made many of their own household items, including mattresses for their beds. Point out that common events such as the death of an old goose and its aftermath are often shown in folk songs. It is this portrayal of everyday life that makes folk songs such a good mirror of history. Teach the children the song by rote and let them sing it as a group while the pictures are displayed again.

Extending Activity: As a follow-up, the entire class or a small group may want to make up additional verses for each of the textless illustrations at the close of the book. Fit the lyrics to the melody and sing the new verses with the original ones Aliki included.

FOLLOW-UP ACTIVITIES FOR TEACHER AND STUDENTS TO SHARE:

1. Introduce Lulu Delacre's *Arroz con Leche* by sharing the illustrations for the song "¡Que llueva! (It's Raining!)," pages 20–21. Ask the children to speculate about the subject of this Puerto Rican song, basing their ideas on the illustration. Share the information below the words on page 21. Sing the song to the children, either in Spanish or English, using the score on page 31. The rhythm pattern may have to be adjusted slightly if the English translation is used. Teach the six-line song by rote.

   In a following lesson teach "Arroz con Leche," pages 14–15, in a similar manner. As the children look at the illustration, tell the class that the view shown here is an actual representation of the Old San

Juan Cathedral in Puerto Rico. Allow the children to play the game described at the bottom of page 14 while they sing the song. For a special treat serve "arroz con leche" (rice with milk). The recipe, in Spanish, is on the title page.

2. Before sharing Peter Spier's *The Fox Went Out on a Chilly Night,* tell the class that the artist pictured an old New England countryside in the illustrations. Ask the children to watch the pictures to see details that let them know the setting depicts long ago rather than recent times. Sing the song for the children while sharing the illustrations. After completing the song, ask the class to identify the things they noticed that led them to assume the song took place long ago. If the children do not call attention to the candles used for lighting, horse-drawn farm machinery, and the covered bridge, point out some of these details and have the children examine the illustrations again. Tell the class they are going to learn the song by rote, repeating a line at a time, because folk songs have traditionally been learned in this manner. Let children discuss how this oral tradition causes folk songs to appear in many forms and variations.

3. Before reading John Langstaff's *Frog Went a-Courtin'*, share the summary of "The Story of This Story" which the author uses as a preface. Tell the class to watch the humorous pictures as they listen to the story. Share the book. While showing the last page of text, ask the children if that page suggests anything else that one might do with the story besides read it. Some child should notice the musical score and suggest that they could sing it. Sing the first verse of the song. Then ask the children to sing the "h'm–h'm" each time it occurs. Sing the entire song, pointing to the children when they are to sing "h'm–h'm." If available, show the sound filmstrip of *Frog Went a-Courtin'* (Weston Woods, 1965, 34 fr., col., 13 min.). Urge the children to sing along with any words they remember until they have mastered as much of the lyrics as desired.

4. Before sharing Peter Spier's *London Bridge Is Falling Down!,* read the section "London Bridge through the Centuries" at the back of the book. Introduce the book to the students by summarizing that section for them. Since many of the children will probably be familiar with the song, it should be easy to teach them to sing the first verse as they examine the first double-spread illustration. Continue the other verses by reciting the first line of each while sharing the appropriate illustration. Have the children sing that verse immediately following the recitation. Complete the eighteen verses by the same process.

As a follow-up have the children think of modern materials that could be suggested in new verses which retain the rhythm of the song. Let the class as a whole decide what could happen if each material were used. As each new verse is created, let the class sing it in unison. Have a committee research in the media center what has happened to the old London Bridge since the publication of Spier's book. Ask them to share their findings with the class.

5. Read *Barn Dance!* by Bill Martin, Jr. and John Archambault. With the help of the physical education teacher, let the children learn a simple square dance set using the lines from the book:

"Right hand! Left hand! Around you go!

Now back-to-back your partners in a do-si-do!

Mules to the center for a curtsey an' a bow!

An' hey there, skinny kid! Show the old cow how!"

6. Introduce *Sally Go Round the Moon* by telling the children that the book contains folk songs from a number of countries and several states in the United States. Locate Ireland on the map or globe. Tell the children that the first song they will learn from the Langstaffs's collection, "Santy Maloney," page 123, comes from Ireland. Teach them the song by rote. After the children have learned the verse, have them sing the song while performing the actions suggested. Let the game continue by making up additional verses as the Langstaffs suggest.

   On another day locate England on the map or globe and introduce the old nursery rhyme "Lavender's Blue," pages 58–59. Teach the children the first verse of the song. When children have mastered the melody and lyrics, introduce the rhythm pattern for the ostinato accompaniment for tuned instruments at the bottom of page 58. Let some children play the ostinato on resonator bells or other tuned instruments as the song is sung again. Then introduce the percussion ostinato. Let the remainder of the class add that pattern on wood blocks or other hand-held percussion instruments to the tuned accompaniment as the class sings. If the children are very advanced and instruments are available, the chime bars part may be added on metallophones, glockenspiels, or other tuned instruments.

7. Introduce the song "The Twelve Days of Christmas" by sharing Jan Brett's illustrated book of the same title. Read or sing the words as the illustrations are shared. Re-examine the illustrations, asking the children to identify the gift given on each of the days. Teach the first

verse of the song by rote. On each of eleven succeeding days teach an additional verse of the cumulative song. As a follow-up, share *Emma's Christmas* by Irene Trivas (Orchard, 1988). Ask children to compare this variant with the traditional *The Twelve Days of Christmas*.

Chapter 6
Music: Fourth Grade/
Fifth Grade

The Mechanics of Music

OBJECTIVES:

1. Participate in the use of multiple voice parts to produce harmony.
2. Recognize that pitch is determined in part by the size and tension of the sound source.
3. Describe the characteristics and development of musical instruments.
4. Explore the nature of sound.

RECOMMENDED READINGS:

Ardley, Neil. *Music.* Illustrated by Dave King, Phillip Dowell, and Michael Dunning. Alfred A. Knopf, 1989.

In two-page illustrated sections Ardley introduces both old and new musical instruments and the theory of sound. (Objectives 3 and 4)

Blocksma, Mary. *The Marvelous Music Machine.* Illustrated by Mischa Richter. Prentice-Hall, 1984.

Black-and-white line drawings and the often humorous text present many unusual facts about the history of the piano and how it works. (Objectives 2 and 3)

Elliott, Donald. *Alligators and Music.* Illustrated by Clinton Arrowood. Gambit, 1976.

With illustrations that show alligators as the musicians, personified instruments of the orchestra introduce themselves. (Objective 3)

Fleischman, Paul. *I Am Phoenix: Poems for Two Voices.* Illustrated by Ken Nutt. Harper & Row, 1985.

With the phrases arranged in two columns to facilitate oral reading, the fifteen poems about birds are enhanced by detailed black-and-white illustrations. (Objective 1)

———. *Joyful Noise: Poems for Two Voices.* Illustrated by Eric Beddows. Harper & Row, 1988.

The phrases of fourteen insect poems designed for two voices are spaced in two columns to facilitate oral reading. (Objective 1)

Kettelkamp, Larry. *The Magic of Sound.* Rev. ed. Illustrated by Anthony Kramer. William Morrow, 1982.

Simple experiments illustrate the concepts of sound and how it is produced. (Objectives 2 and 4)

Newman, Frederick R. *MouthSounds.* Workman, 1980.

This manual gives directions for creating over 70 sounds with the human mouth and includes a recording of each sound. (Objective 4)

Walther, Tom. *Make Mine Music!* Little, Brown, 1981.

Following a discussion of the principles of sound, musical instruments are described and directions are given for making and playing them. (Objectives 3 and 4)

GROUP INTRODUCTORY ACTIVITY:

Preparation: Locate Tom Walther's *Make Mine Music!* and prepare a sound quiz in which the children must match the sound and the source, as suggested on page 11 of Walther's book.

Focus: Distribute the quiz and give the children time to complete it.

Objective: In order to satisfy the objectives of exploring the nature of sound and describing the characteristics and development of musical instruments, carry out the guided activity.

Guided Activity: Check the answers to the sound quiz the children took and let the class make the sounds included on the quiz. Then ask the children to sit quietly with their eyes closed and listen for sounds around them. Next have each child list on the back of the quiz paper the sounds he or she heard. Write the sounds on the board to see if some children noticed sounds others did not hear.

Read to the children the section "A Sound Is Worth a Thousand Words" from Walther's book, page 11. Tell the children that now they are going to discover "idiophones." After sharing page 56, explain to the children that the word "naturally" is very important in the definition of an idiophone. For example, only when it is stretched taut can a plucked guitar string make a sound. It does not make a sound in its natural state. Demonstrate this by plucking at a string lying loose on the desk.

Extending Activity: Tell the children to go home and make or find an idiophone to share with the class on the following day. On the next day, after each student has demonstrated his or her idiophone, ask the children in which orchestral family the idiophones would belong. If no student responds correctly, point out that idiophones are consistent with the nature of percussion instruments. Display a maracca and a drum and ask the children what natural idiophones make a similar sound, e.g., dried seed pods and hollow logs. Tell the children they may want to read portions of the book and share other musical activities with their friends.

FOLLOW-UP ACTIVITIES FOR TEACHER AND STUDENTS TO SHARE:

1. Introduce Neil Ardley's *Music* by sharing pages 6–7, "Seeing Sound," with the students. Point out the peaks of the illustrated soundwaves created by the tuning fork, violin, and flute. Note that all three soundwaves represent the same pitch. This is indicated by the equal distance between the peaks of the waves from each source. Read to the class the small print descriptions of each of the four soundwaves. Show the class some of the illustrations of old and new instruments in the book. Suggest that they may want to do an individual activity and place their responses on a "Did You Know?" bulletin board.

2. Introduce Mary Blocksma's *The Marvelous Music Machine* by asking the question, "How is a piano like a motorcycle?" After children have tried to guess, share the answer from the third page of the section on strings. Read to the class the pages on "The Strings" that precede the motorcycle question (the book is unpaginated but sections are labeled in bold type). Let the children discuss facts they learned about pitch and volume (dynamics). Tell the students that the book will be placed in the reading area. Assign short segments for each child to read so they can share an interesting fact about the piano with the class.

3. Introduce Donald Elliott's *Alligators and Music* by reading sections of the text describing the oboes, the tuba, and the triangle. Let the children discuss the character of each personified instrument. How does each instrument feel about its role in the orchestra? Ask the class in which family of instruments each one described belongs. What other instruments belong to each family? Ask each member of the class to select one instrument that was named and write a paragraph about how that instrument describes and feels about itself. After the paragraph is completed, let each child compare the written paragraph with Elliott's description.

4. Before sharing Paul Fleischman's *Joyful Noise: Poems for Two Voices,* practice the poem "Cicadas," pages 26–28, with a student or teacher. Prepare students to experience these two-voice poems by introducing the term "quodlibet" as a composition that combines two songs with different words and melodies sung simultaneously. (Quodlibets are often called simply "partner songs," and that term may be substituted, if desired.) Play for the children a recording of a quodlibet such as Bing and Gary Crosby's "Play a Simple Melody" (*The Best of Bing Crosby,* MCA, MCAC2-4045, 1 cs). Then explain to the class that *Joyful Noise* by Paul Fleischman is a collection of poems for two voices. Read Fleischman's "Note" which follows the "Contents." Tell the students to listen carefully because at different times the voices alternate, speak in chorus, echo each other, or say different words simultaneously as in a quodlibet. Read "Cicadas" with the partner. Assign partners and poems in the book for students to practice and present to the class on a later date.

5. Collect five various-sized drinking glasses and place them on the desk. Ask a student to tap the glasses lightly with a pencil. Let the class help him or her arrange the glasses in a row according to ascending pitch. When the glasses are correctly arranged, ask the children to speculate about why the glasses have different pitches. Read the two sentences that precede the described experiment on pages 22–23 of Larry Kettelkamp's *The Magic of Sound.* Tell the children that Kettelkamp's book includes many simple experiments relating to the principles of sound which they may want to carry out.

FOLLOW-UP ACTIVITIES FOR INDIVIDUAL STUDENTS:

1. After being introduced to Neil Ardley's *Music* in class, choose one of the two-page sections about old or new musical instruments that interests you. Read the segment and make a list of six interesting facts you learned. Decorate your page with an appropriate border and place it on the "Did You Know?" bulletin board.

2. After experiencing quodlibets and hearing two-voice poems from Paul Fleischman's *Joyful Noise* shared in class, choose a partner and select a poem from *I Am Phoenix*, Fleischman's first book of poetry for two voices. Practice the poem with your partner and read it aloud to the class.

3. After sharing the experiment involving the pitch of drinking glasses from Larry Kettelkamp's *The Magic of Sound,* select and read about another experiment in the book relating to sound. If you wish to demonstrate the experiment to the class, be sure to identify the principle of sound that it illustrates.

4. After having shared Neil Ardley's *Music* in class, listen to "Introduction and Principles of Mouthsounds," the first section of the recording that accompanies Frederick Newman's *MouthSounds*. Now listen to the section "Musical Instruments" from the same recording. Examine the book and select a type of musical instrument from chapter six that you would like to interpret with your mouth. Read the directions and practice the sound. When you feel you have mastered the mouthsound, share it with the class. You may wish to form a "Mouthsounds Band" with several friends. Each may choose and perfect a different musical mouthsound and perform together.

Form and Style

OBJECTIVES:

1. Recognize the jazz idiom.
2. Distinguish between program music and absolute music (music that tells a story versus music for its own sake).
3. Experience spirituals.
4. Identify opera, ballet, and musical comedy as forms of music theater.
5. Learn patriotic or folk songs and the historical context of each.

RECOMMENDED READINGS:

Bangs, Edward. *Yankee Doodle.* Illustrated by Steven Kellogg. Four Winds, 1976, 1980.
After presenting the historical background of the song, highly detailed illustrations portray both the lyrics and a humorous subplot. (Objective 5)

Crespi, Francesca. *The Magic Flute: The Story of Mozart's Opera.* Retold by Margaret Greaves. Henry Holt, 1989.
Illustrations enhance the story of the popular opera which was Mozart's last work. (Objective 4)

The Erie Canal. Illustrated by Peter Spier. Doubleday, 1970.
A history of the Erie Canal is included in this illustrated version of the American folk song. (Objective 5)

Fleischman, Paul. *Rondo in C.* Illustrated by Janet Wentworth. Harper & Row, 1988.
Illustrations depict the individual reactions of members of the audience as a young girl plays Beethoven's "Rondo in C" on the piano. (Objective 2)

Fonteyn, Margot. *Swan Lake.* Illustrated by Trina Schart Hyman. Harcourt Brace Jovanovich, 1989.
Lavish illustrations enhance the prima ballerina Margot Fonteyn's retelling of the classic ballet *Swan Lake.* (Objective 4)

Go In and Out the Window. Illustrations from the collection of The Metropolitan Museum of Art. Henry Holt, 1987.
Sixty-one traditional songs, with musical scores and comments on the music and artwork included, are illustrated by reproductions of treasures from The Metropolitan Museum of Art. (Objectives 3 and 5)

Gregory, Cynthia. *Cynthia Gregory Dances Swan Lake.* Illustrated by Martha Swope. Simon & Schuster, 1990.
Photographs aid young people in picturing the events of the day in which ballerina Cynthia Gregory performs *Swan Lake.* (Objective 4)

Hughes, Langston. *Jazz.* Franklin Watts, 1982.
This introduction to jazz includes both its historical development and some of its famous performers. (Objective 1)

Isadora, Rachel. *Ben's Trumpet.* Greenwillow, 1979.
Text and illustrations combine to emphasize the fascination young Ben feels for the trumpet and its jazz music. (Objectives 1 and 2)

Key, Francis Scott. *The Star-Spangled Banner.* Illustrated by Peter Spier. Doubleday, 1973.
Illustrations depicting both historical and modern scenes extend the lyrics of the national anthem, followed by the history of the War of 1812 and by the musical score. (Objective 5)

Komaiko, Leah. *I Like the Music.* Illustrated by Barbara Westman. Harper & Row, 1987.

A young girl prefers the "found" music of the street to the symphony her grandmother loves, but both find common ground at an outdoor concert. (Objective 2)

The Laura Ingalls Wilder Songbook. Compiled by Eugenia Garson. Illustrated by Garth Williams. Harper & Row, 1968.

Music for 62 songs Pa sang or played are notated along with brief notes and references to the specific pages on which the song appears in Wilder's Little House books. (Objective 5)

Powers, Bill. *Behind the Scenes of a Broadway Musical.* Crown, 1982.

Black-and-white photographs extend the text which describes many aspects of the Broadway musical *Really Rosie.* (Objective 4)

Price, Leontyne. *Aida.* Illustrated by Leo and Diane Dillon. Harcourt Brace Jovanovich, 1990.

Illustrated by vibrant paintings, Verdi's *Aida* is retold by one closely identified with the role. (Objective 4)

Rosenberg, Jane. *Sing Me a Story.* Thames and Hudson, 1989.

Following the introduction by Luciano Pavarotti, the stories of fifteen operas are presented. (Objective 4)

Schroeder, Alan. *Ragtime Tumpie.* Illustrated by Bernie Fuchs. Little, Brown, 1989.

Tumpie's love of jazz compels her to dance in this fictionalized account of the childhood of the legendary Josephine Baker. (Objective 1)

Spruyt, E. Lee. *Behind the Golden Curtain.* Four Winds, 1986.

Glowing illustrations highlight the many backstage activities involved in the presentation of *Hansel and Gretel* at the Metropolitan Opera House. (Objective 4)

Tusa, Tricia. *Miranda.* Macmillan, 1985.

Young Miranda refuses to play the piano after adults complain about her "boogie-woogie." (Objective 1)

What a Morning! Edited by John Langstaff. Illustrated by Ashley Bryan. Macmillan, 1987.

Five Christmas spirituals with piano scores are vividly illustrated in tempera. (Objective 3)

GROUP INTRODUCTORY ACTIVITY:

Preparation: Locate *The Laura Ingalls Wilder Songbook*, compiled by Eugenia Garson, and find Laura Ingalls Wilder's *On the Banks of Plum Creek*. Prepare a transparency with the words to "Wait for the Wagon" *(The Laura Ingalls Wilder Songbook*, pages 108–109) or write the words on the chalkboard.

Focus: Introduce *The Laura Ingalls Wilder Songbook* by covering the title page and showing the Garth Williams illustration on the facing page. Ask the children if anyone knows what book character the drawing depicts. If no one responds, ask the children if any of them have read Laura Ingalls Wilder's *Little House in the Big Woods* or another book in the series. Tell the children that *The Laura Ingalls Wilder Songbook* contains the musical scores of 62 songs mentioned in Wilder's stories of her childhood.

Objective: In order to fulfill the objectives of learning patriotic and folk songs and the historical context of each, read the first page of Eugenia Garson's preface which describes the role of music in the lives of pioneers.

Guided Activity: Display the words of "Wait for the Wagon" on the chalkboard or overhead projector. Teach the melody of the song by rote. Let the students sing the song. Then read the excerpt about Pa's singing the song, described on page 181 of Wilder's *On the Banks of Plum Creek*. Let children discuss why they think Ma did not want Pa to sing "Wait for the Wagon" on Sunday.

Extending Activity: On succeeding days choose other folk or patriotic songs from the book that come from the pioneer period, such as "The Girl I Left Behind Me," pages 112–113, or "When Johnny Comes Marching Home Again," pages 82–83. Teach the songs in a similar manner, being sure to share the excerpt from the appropriate Laura Ingalls Wilder book.

FOLLOW-UP ACTIVITIES FOR TEACHER AND STUDENTS TO SHARE:

1. Introduce Edward Bangs's *Yankee Doodle,* illustrated by Steven Kellogg, through sharing the history of the song given on the first page of text. Because the intricate illustrations are difficult to see in

a large class group, show the Weston Woods sound filmstrip version of the book (SF173C, 1976, 53 fr, col., 1 cs, 10 min). View the filmstrip again, pausing to discuss unfamiliar phrases in the lyrics. Sing the first verse of the song and teach additional verses as desired.

2. Play excerpts from Mozart's *The Magic Flute* (RCA, RCD1-4621, 1 cd) in the background while reading the story from Francesca Crespi's illustrated book of the same title. After completing the book, play Papageno's song, asking students to notice how Mozart's melody mimics the song of a bird because Papageno was a bird-catcher by trade. Tell the students that this selection is one of the most familiar passages from the opera. As a follow-up, invite a flautist from the local high school or community orchestra to visit the class and play for the children. Suggest that the flautist share a piece of music that exhibits the songbird quality of the flute, such as the bird theme from Prokofiev's *Peter and the Wolf* or an excerpt from *The Magic Flute.*

3. Introduce Peter Spier's *The Erie Canal* by sharing the small map at the back of the book and by locating Albany and Buffalo, New York, on a wall map. Read to the class the history of the Erie Canal from the back of the book. As each question is read, give children an opportunity to speculate upon possible answers before reading Spier's response. Read the first verse, showing the children the pictures. Then sing the melody included in the score at the end of the book. Teach the class the melody by rote, sharing the appropriate illustrations. When children are secure in the melody for the verse, teach the chorus in the same manner. Continue the book, singing the second verse as the pictures are shared. Have the children join in on the chorus. As a follow-up, sing the song again, letting a few of the children use woodblocks or temple blocks to play a "clip clop" rhythm pattern to represent the mule's hooves as the barge is pulled through the canal.

4. Remind students that the definition of program music is music that tells a story through sound alone, with no words. Read Paul Fleischman's *Rondo in C.* After completing the book, ask the students what story the music "Rondo in C" tells. After a few moments of waiting, tell the children that they can not give an answer to the question because "Rondo in C" does not tell a story. Explain to the students that Beethoven's "Rondo in C" is not program music. Instead, it is "absolute music," i.e., music for its own sake. Point out that this type of music lets each listener react to the sound in his or her own way. This explains the different expressions on the faces of the audience that are illustrated in Fleischman's book.

As a follow-up, play a recording of Beethoven's "Rondo in C" (*Concertos for Pianoforte and Orchestra*, Progressive Records, D-175, 1 cd) or another Beethoven piano piece such as "Moonlight Sonata" (*Rubenstein Plays Three Favorite Beethoven Sonatas*, RCA, ARK1-4001, 1 cs). Play the piece again, asking students to draw a picture illustrating what they think of when they hear the music.

5. Introduce *Swan Lake* by explaining to the class that this is the story of Peter Ilyich Tchaikovsky's famous ballet. It has been retold by Margot Fonteyn, a ballerina who has danced *Swan Lake* hundreds of times. Before sharing in class, read the "Storyteller's Note on the Ballet" at the end of the book and the note about Dame Margot Fonteyn on the book jacket. Select a few facts about the ballet and Dame Fonteyn to share with the class. Read *Swan Lake,* allowing time for the students to enjoy Trina Schart Hyman's illustrations. After sharing the book, encourage children to discuss their favorite scenes.

   As a follow-up, play excerpts from Peter Ilyich Tchaikovsky's *Story of Swan Lake* (Caedmon, 1981, 2s, 12 in, 33 rpm, 61 min) that correspond to favorite scenes identified by the children. Claire Bloom's reading of the story will expedite finding the appropriate scenes. Ask children to listen carefully to the music and visualize the dancers in the ballet. To introduce an individual activity for ballet, read the final paragraph of the first page of text from *Cynthia Gregory Dances Swan Lake* by Cynthia Gregory. Urge children who are interested in ballet to complete the individual activity.

6. Introduce *Go In and Out the Window* by sharing the reproduction of "The Coming Storm" by Martin Johnson Heade on page 33. Read the explanation of the painting on pages 33–34 which also explains spirituals. Sing "Down by the Riverside" from pages 33–35 for the class, asking them to clap the steady beat when the chorus is sung. Teach the chorus by rote and sing the song again, urging the children to sing the parts of the verse that they recall and all join in singing the chorus. By the time the song has been sung three or four times, most children should be participating in the entire performance. On a following day teach the spiritual "Nobody Knows the Trouble I've Seen," pages 89–90, sharing the illustration of "July Hay" by Thomas Hart Benton and the interpretation of it. If possible, invite a local baritone to visit the class and sing some spirituals for the children.

On another day share some of the American folk songs in the book that are not spirituals. Teach "Home on the Range," pages 56–59. Ask a student or a committee to go to the media center and find out which state has adopted this song as their official state song (Kansas). Let the student or group report their findings to the class. On a subsequent day teach the children "Shenandoah," pages 118–119. Introduce the song by sharing the illustration of "Fur Traders Descending the Missouri" by George Caleb Bingham. Read to the class the accompanying history of the song and the painting.

7. As Rachel Isadora's story *Ben's Trumpet* is read aloud, play as background music the Louis Armstrong performance from Langston Hughes's *The Story of Jazz* (Smithsonian Folkways, distributed by Rounder Records, FC 7312, 1 cs) or another Armstrong recording. Let children discuss why the illustrations so often show sharp angles and zig-zag lines. Someone should deduce that these lines are reminescent of the jerky rhythm and syncopation common to jazz. Have the children speculate on the future of Ben. Tell students that the music that was played as a background to the story was performed by Louis Armstrong, one of the most famous jazz trumpet players. Play the music again, having children listen closely to feel the rhythm of the music. Urge the children to discuss why music of this type might appeal to Ben.

8. Have the students sing the first verse of "The Star-Spangled Banner." Then tell them that Peter Spier has illustrated all the verses of the national anthem of the United States in his book *The Star-Spangled Banner*. Ask the children to watch the illustrations carefully to see if there are any locations they recognize. After completing the book, turn back to locate any illustrations the children wish to discuss. As a follow-up, ask the students to each make a list of four places or scenes in their home state that they feel could be used to illustrate "the land of the free and the home of the brave." Compile a class list on butcher paper and post with the title "The Land of the Free and the Home of the Brave."

9. Read Leah Komaiko's *I Like the Music*. Discuss "found music," music that occurs naturally in the environment or sounds produced from everyday objects. Have children find objects in the classroom or at home that can be used to create sounds. Let the students use these to create found music to match the rhythm of the poetry on the pages beginning with, "But I like the music in the street. . . ," "I like the beat," and "When they sing. . . ." Practice until the rhythms are

compatible. Read the story again with a student acting as the conductor to show student musicians when to enter and stop each time. Let students select a recording of traditional symphonic music to use as background for the pages referring to the symphony. Combine the traditional music with the found music for the conclusion, beginning with "I like the music late at night." Tape record the final product and place the book and tape in a listening station in the school media center.

10. Before sharing chapter four from *Behind the Scenes of a Broadway Musical* by Bill Powers, tell the children that they will see a videotape of the original, animated version of Maurice Sendak's *Really Rosie* (Weston Woods, 1983, 26 min.). Point out that the music was written by singer-songwriter Carole King and the lyrics were by Maurice Sendak. Explain that many of the lyrics were based on five of Sendak's books for children. After viewing the video, tell the children that this animated television special was expanded into a Broadway musical. Let the children speculate upon changes that would be necessary in order to perform *Really Rosie* on stage with live actors.

Read Powers's chapter "The Music" to the class. Ask the children to recall the steps in preparing the music for the production. Compare these steps to comments the students may have made during the speculation period. Tell the children that all stages of preparing the musical are included in the book by Powers. Ask for volunteers to read each of the other chapters in the book from "Planning the Play" to "Opening Night." Have these children share a brief summary of the chapters at a later date by each showing five illustrations from the chapter and describing what each photograph depicts.

11. Introduce *Aida* by telling the children that Leontyne Price, who wrote this retelling of Giuseppi Verdi's opera, is an opera star herself. Her most famous role was Aida and her interpretation is recognized as a model for others. Point out both Egypt and Ethiopia on the map. Tell the children that this is the story of an Ethiopian princess and an Egyptian general. Explain that it is said that *Aida* was based on an actual incident brought to light during an archeological dig in Egypt. Read the book to the students, sharing the illustrations by the Dillons. Call attention to the borders, metal frames designed and created by Leo and Diane Dillon's son, Lee. After completing the book, give the children an opportunity to comment on the story. Lead them to discuss events in the story that would create drama on the stage.

Play "The Triumphal Entry" from *Aida* (RCA, RK-1237, 1 cs) for the class. Do not tell children the title of the work, but instead ask them to listen carefully and determine where in the story they think this music might occur. After hearing the march, let the children discuss their ideas about what part of the story the music represents. If no one suggests the return of Radames and his victorious army, give them that information.

As a follow-up, ask two small committees of children to go to the library media center. One group is to find information on the life of the composer Verdi to share with the class. Ask the other group to see if they can find information on other operas written by Verdi.

12. Introduce Jane Rosenberg's *Sing Me a Story* by reading Luciano Pavarotti's introduction in which he discusses the nature of opera and the value of being introduced to the stories prior to hearing the music. Tell the children that the book will be placed in the reading area where they may choose to read the story of one of the operas in the book. Ask the children to draw a picture of a stage setting for a favorite scene that is not illustrated in Rosenberg's book. Then the students may show their illustrations to the class and give a very brief synopsis of the opera's plot.

13. Play a portion of "The Entertainer" (*The Best of Scott Joplin*, Vanguard, CVSD-39-40, 2 cs) or another recording of a Scott Joplin tune or other ragtime music. Tell the children that Alan Schroeder's *Ragtime Tumpie* is the story of the dancer Josephine Baker who loved to dance to jazz music such as they have been hearing. Read *Ragtime Tumpie* to the class. As a follow-up, have the children research in the media center the terms "ragtime" and "syncopation." Ask an accomplished pianist to play "Chicken Chowder" from the endpapers of the book while children listen for examples of syncopation in the song. Have children clap or tap the rhythm of the syncopated patterns they identify. Urge the children to do one of the individual follow-up activities on jazz.

14. Read Tricia Tusa's *Miranda* to the class. Then let the children discuss why the adults did not want her to play "boogie-woogie" music. Ask the students if anyone has an idea of what "boogie-woogie" is. Play "The Boogie-Woogie Bugle Boy " (*Legendary Performers*, RCA, CRK1-2064, 1 cs) for the class and have children discuss why Miranda might have preferred this type of music, which is a derivative of the jazz idiom.

15. Before sharing *What a Morning!* read John Langstaff's "Note to Teachers. . ." on the last page. Tell children that African American spirituals are often religious because many of the slaves who originated these songs found hope and comfort in Bible stories. Play on the piano the chorus of "Go Tell It on the Mountain" and see if anyone can identify the title. Teach the chorus of the song to the class. Sing the verses and have the students join in on the chorus. Before sharing Ashley Bryan's illustrations, have children prepare an illustration for the song using the medium of their choice. On a succeeding day share "Mary Had a Baby" as an example of the call and response form common in many spirituals. The children may write additional lines for the song as Langstaff suggests.

FOLLOW-UP ACTIVITIES FOR INDIVIDUAL STUDENTS:

1. After sharing *Yankee Doodle* in class, examine Steven Kellogg's illustrated book in the reading area. Notice the subplot about the little boy. Write a paragraph describing the action that is not mentioned in the words of the song. How does Steven Kellogg illustrate Jemima?
2. After sharing Dame Margot Fonteyn's *Swan Lake* in class, read *Cynthia Gregory Dances Swan Lake.* Write a paragraph describing the hard work and problems involved in being a ballet dancer.
3. After sharing *Swan Lake* by Margot Fonteyn in class, read *Cynthia Gregory Dances Swan Lake.* List five reasons why someone would enjoy being a ballet dancer.
4. After hearing Alan Schroeder's *Ragtime Tumpie*, read Langston Hughes's *Jazz.* Share with the class what you feel to be the most important steps in the development of the jazz style.
5. After having shared Leontyne Price's *Aida* in class, read *Behind the Golden Curtain* by E. Lee Spruyt. Choose three favorite illustrations of backstage activities and share them with the class. Describe each illustration and how the costumes, sets, or special effects depicted contributed to the effectiveness of the presentation of the opera *Hansel and Gretel.*
6. After sharing Tricia Tusa's *Miranda* in class, ask your grandparent or a senior citizen if he or she recalls the title of any boogie-woogie music and memories of when or where it was played or heard. Record your findings and share them with the class.

Composers and Musicians

OBJECTIVES:

1. Realize that a composer's music reflects his or her life and times.
2. Identify major American composers and musicians.
3. Recognize the major composers of traditional music.

RECOMMENDED READINGS:

Ardley, Neil. *Music: An Illustrated Encyclopedia.* Facts on File, 1986.
    Brief biographical sketches of composers and musicians are included in
    this illustrated reference work. (Objectives 1, 2, and 3)
Brighton, Catherine. *Mozart: Scenes from the Childhood of the Great
    Composer.* Doubleday, 1990.
    This illustrated, episodic biography highlights events in the life of
    Mozart and his sister. (Objectives 1 and 3)
Greene, Carol. *Ludwig van Beethoven: Musical Pioneer.* Children's Press,
    1989.
    This brief, illustrated biography highlights major events in the composer's
    stormy life. (Objectives 1 and 3)
Iverson, Genie. *Louis Armstrong.* Crowell, 1976.
    This short biography details Armstrong's early life and its influence on
    his musical career. (Objective 2)
Lasker, David. *The Boy Who Loved Music.* Illustrated by Joe Lasker.
    Viking, 1979.
    Striking illustrations lend historical authenticity to this fictionalized
    account of the composition of Joseph Haydn's "Farewell" Symphony
    (*#45 in F# Minor*). (Objectives 1 and 3)
Lepscky, Ibi. *Amadeus Mozart.* Illustrated by Paolo Cardoni. Barron's,
    1982.
    This illustrated biography of the famous composer focuses on his
    childhood. (Objectives 1 and 3)
Mitchell, Barbara. *America, I Hear You: A Story About George Gershwin.*
    Carolrhoda, 1987.
    In a brief biography the important events associated with each of
    Gershwin's major compositions are presented. (Objectives 1 and 2)

Montgomery, Elizabeth Rider. *Duke Ellington: King of Jazz.* Illustrated by Paul Frame. Garrard, 1972.
This biography of a jazz great shares the conflict Ellington felt in choosing between art and music as a career. (Objective 2)

Stevens, Bryna. *Handel and the Famous Sword Swallower of Halle.* Illustrated by Ruth Tietjen Councell. Philomel, 1990.
This illustrated biography recounts George Frederick Handel's boyhood determination to study music. (Objectives 1 and 3)

Terkel, Studs. *Giants of Jazz.* Rev. ed. Crowell, 1975.
Brief biographies of thirteen well-known jazz musicians highlight their lives and music. (Objectives 1 and 2)

Ventura, Piero. *Great Composers.* G.P. Putnam's Sons, 1989.
Composers from a number of centuries are briefly shared and their contributions to music are identified. (Objectives 1 and 3)

GROUP INTRODUCTORY ACTIVITY:

Preparation: Locate David Lasker's *The Boy Who Loved Music* and a recording of Joseph Haydn's *Symphony #45 in F# Minor,* "Farewell" (Columbia, MPT-39068, 1cs).

Focus: Introduce David Lasker's *The Boy Who Loved Music* by reading to the class the introductory note about musicians in eighteenth-century Europe.

Objective: To satisfy the objective of realizing that a composer's music reflects his or her life and times and of recognizing major composers of traditional music, share with the class David Lasker's *The Boy Who Loved Music* and Joseph Haydn's "Farewell" Symphony.

Guided Activity: Read David Lasker's *The Boy Who Loved Music* to the class. Then, because the illustrations authentically depict the historical setting, go back and have students retell the story from the illustrations.

Extending Activity: Play excerpts from Joseph Haydn's "Farewell" Symphony, including the final movement in which the players leave the stage. Let students discuss how Prince Nicolaus must have felt as he watched the musicians leave one by one. Can the children think of reactions the Prince might have shown other than congratulating Haydn and allowing the musicians to go home the next day? What might have happened if the Prince had been angered by the performance?

FOLLOW-UP ACTIVITIES FOR TEACHER AND STUDENTS TO SHARE:

1. To introduce the composer Wolfgang Amadeus Mozart, locate on a map of Austria the cities of Salzburg, his childhood home, and Vienna, where his family later moved. Share the cover of Catherine Brighton's *Mozart*. Tell the children that Brighton traveled to Salzburg and other cities important in Mozart's early life in order to do extensive research. This research allowed her to accurately create the illustrations for the book. Share the illustrations as the first portion of the book is read, stopping after reading the excerpt entitled "Chelsea." Then play an excerpt from a Mozart symphony, such as *Symphony #41 in C Major, K. 551*, "Jupiter" (Columbia, YT 35493, 1 cs). Remind children that Mozart wrote his first orchestral music when he was younger than the students in the class. On the following day, complete Brighton's work and the summary of Mozart's later life found on the endpapers. Play another excerpt from a Mozart composition, such as *Eine Kleine Nachtmusik (Mozart's Greatest Hits*, Columbia, COL MG-31267, 4s, 12in., 33rpm).

   As a follow-up, ask the children if any of them take piano lessons. If some do, ask them to see if there is a Mozart piece included in their piano books. If so, suggest that they practice it and play the music for the class. If no student is capable of sharing Mozart, have an accomplished pianist or other musician visit and play a brief Mozart selection for the class.

2. Read to the class Carol Greene's *Ludwig van Beethoven: Musical Pioneer*. Discuss with the class how events in Beethoven's life were reflected in his music, e.g., his happiness during his early years in Vienna produced light, joyous pieces. Have the children speculate about Beethoven's emotions when he realized he was losing his hearing. Do they think those feelings might have been expressed in his music? Play excerpts from well-known Beethoven compositions, including *Symphony #9 in D Minor, Op. 125*, "Choral" (Columbia, COL MY-37241, 2s, 12in., 33rpm). Remind the children that this symphony was written and performed after Beethoven was almost deaf. Point out that the "Choral" Symphony is the work that was discussed in chapter five of Carol Greene's book. If any of the students play piano and have a Beethoven piece available, they may want to perform the music for the class.

3. Before reading Genie Iverson's *Louis Armstrong* to the class, ask the children to listen carefully for interesting bits of information about this famous American musician. After completing the book, let children discuss interesting facts they remember, such as how he got the nickname "Satchmo" and how he learned to play the cornet. As a follow-up, play a recording of Louis Armstrong, such as "Hello Dolly" (MCA, MCA-538, 2s, 12in., 33rpm), in which he both sings and plays cornet.

4. Ask the media specialist to locate additional copies of Barbara Mitchell's *America, I Hear You* through interlibrary loan. Assign a small group of interested students to read the biography and share the information with the class through a panel discussion. Ask the children to be sure they focus on the events that inspired each of Gershwin's major works. Following the panel discussion, play excerpts from George Gershwin's best known works, including "Rhapsody in Blue" and *Porgy and Bess* (*Gershwin's Greatest Hits*, RCA, RK-1184, 1 cs).

5. Introduce composer George Frederick Handel by sharing Bryna Stevens's *Handel and the Famous Sword Swallower of Halle*. Read the book to the class, sharing the illustrations. After completing the book, let the children discuss the differences between Handel's life and their lives today. Let children recall interesting facts about Handel's early life and his desire to be a musician. Play excerpts from Handel's *Water Music Suite* or *Royal Fireworks Music* (Vanguard, VBD-71176, 1cd). On the following day play brief excerpts from *The Messiah* (RCA, AGK1-5227, 1 cs), including "The Hallelujah Chorus." Tell the children that this piece contains the music for which Handel is probably most well-known. Explain that a king of England attended an early performance of *The Messiah*. When "The Hallelujah Chorus" was performed, the king was so moved that he rose to his feet. Since the law forbade anyone to sit when the king was standing, everyone in the room stood also. Thanks to this incident, it is still a popular practice for the audience to stand during the singing of "The Hallelujah Chorus."

FOLLOW-UP ACTIVITIES FOR INDIVIDUAL STUDENTS:

1. After hearing in class about the lives of several composers, select one of those presented. Using Neil Ardley's *Music: An Illustrated Encyclopedia,* see if you can locate and list at least one fact about that composer that was not presented in class.

2. After having shared the stories of Louis Armstrong and George Gershwin in class, read the chapter "Popular Music," pages 102–121, in Neil Ardley's *Music: An Illustrated Encyclopedia.* Select five American composers or musicians who you believe made a significant contribution to the music of their times. Document your choice by describing the contributions of each.

3. After sharing in class Catherine Brighton's *Mozart: Scenes from the Childhood of the Great Composer,* read *Amadeus Mozart* by Ibi Lepscky. Write a paragraph evaluating which of the two books you feel presented Mozart's early life most vividly. Which gave you a better feeling of the times in which he lived? Document your decision.

4. After having heard Genie Iverson's *Louis Armstrong,* read Elizabeth Montgomery's *Duke Ellington: King of Jazz.* Write a paragraph about Ellington's difficult choice in selecting a career. Share your paragraph with the class if time allows.

5. After hearing Genie Iverson's *Louis Armstrong,* read a biography of a famous American musician such as Duke Ellington or Benny Goodman from Studs Terkel's *Giants of Jazz.* List ten interesting facts about the musician that you could share with the class. Check with your music teacher, school or public librarian, a parent, or another adult to find a recording of music by the artist you chose. Play a portion of the music as you share the information with the class.

6. After sharing Catherine Brighton's *Mozart* and Bryna Steven's *Handel and the Famous Sword Swallower of Halle* in class, select three composers from the Table of Contents in Piero Ventura's *Great Composers.* Turn to the indicated page and read the short biographical sketch about each. List the three facts you found most interesting about each composer.

Index

by Linda Webster